CHARLES A. LINDBERGH

Recent Titles in
Popular Culture Bio-Bibliographies: A Reference Series
Series Editor: M. Thomas Inge

CHARLES A. LINDBERGH
A Bio-Bibliography

Perry D. Luckett

Popular Culture Bio-Bibliographies

Greenwood Press
New York • Westport, Connecticut • London

Library of Congress Cataloging-in-Publication Data

Luckett, Perry D.
  Charles A. Lindbergh, a bio-bibliography.

  (Popular culture bio-bibliographies, ISSN 0193-6891)
  Bibliography: p.
  Includes index.
  1. Lindbergh, Charles A. (Charles Augustus), 1902-
1974. 2. Lindbergh, Charles A. (Charles Augustus),
1902-1974—Bibliography. 3. Air pilots—United States—
Biography. I. Title.
TL540.L5L83 1986   619.13'092'4 [B]   86-3165
ISBN 0-313-23098-6 (lib. bdg. : alk. paper)

Library of Congress Catalog Card Number: 86-3165
ISBN: 0-313-23098-6
ISSN: 0193-6891

First published in 1986

Greenwood Press, Inc.
88 Post Road West, Westport, Connecticut 06881

Printed in the United States of America

The paper used in this book complies with the
Permanent Paper Standard issued by the National
Information Standards Organization (Z39.48-1984).

10 9 8 7 6 5 4 3 2 1

For
Irene, Sean, and Colleen
in patience and love

CONTENTS

ILLUSTRATIONS

ACKNOWLEDGMENTS

I am grateful to several people who made this book more accurate and thorough. Chuck Stone, manager of the Lindbergh Historic Site at Little Falls, Minnesota, introduced me to Lindbergh's formative life and surroundings and allowed me to consult documents at the Site. Judith Schiff, archivist at Yale University's Sterling Memorial Library, provided me with a manuscript copy of Truman Smith's report on air intelligence activities in Germany during the late 1930s; it gave me special insight into Lindbergh's contributions to pre-World War II military preparations. Duane Reed and Don Barrett, of the U.S. Air Force Academy's Special Collections Branch, were especially gracious in showing me sheet music, memorabilia, bibliographies, and original manuscript letters concerning Lindbergh's career.

Original illustrations of Lindbergh's transatlantic and other exploratory flights, as well as the line drawing of the *Spirit of St. Louis*, were done by Tanya Rosburg, based on similar illustrations in the *Lindbergh Historical Site Instructor's Guide*, compiled by Lori Nelson and published in 1982 by the Minnesota Historical Society.

I'm indebted to John Stanaway, John R. Ferguson, Chuck Stone, and the Lindbergh Historic Site for permission to use some photographs: Charles Lindbergh and Tommy McGuire or Joe Foss in the South Pacific in 1944, and Lindbergh at his mother's dining room table in the restored home at Little Falls, Minnesota. For permission to print six other photographs of Lindbergh and of his receptions after the transatlantic flight, I'm grateful to the National Air and Space Museum, Smithsonian Institution, in Washington, D.C. Each of these photographs is separately credited in the text.

I'm also especially indebted to my editors for their support, sensitivity, and erudition. Marilyn Brownstein guided early research. M. Thomas

Inge, of Randolph-Macon College in Ashland, Virginia, read and commented upon the entire manuscript. And Cynthia Harris patiently guided me through two years of research and writing to produce this book in its present form. Much of the credit for its quality belongs to them; any errors in its content or misinterpretations are, of course, my own.

1

A LINDBERGH LIFE

When Charles A. Lindbergh shocked the world with his transatlantic flight in 1927, people marked him as a brash young Lochinvar, riding out of the west to bring a jaded world courage and heroic action.[1] Typecasting continued in reams of newsprint, radio broadcasts, and film. Soon, Lindbergh was subsumed into this image of mythic hero. Obscure origins, itinerant youth (as a stuntman and barnstormer), selective education for action, and sudden catapult into greatness or fame—this is the stuff of Joseph Campbell's *The Hero With a Thousand Faces*, with precedents like Christ, Beowulf, and Shakespeare's Henry V.[2] But the brief biography that follows shows Lindbergh was at once different from and more complex than this archetypal figure.

FAMILY BACKGROUND

Charles was born the only son of Congressman Charles August (C. A.) Lindbergh and Evangeline Lodge Land. Each family contributed significantly to his upbringing. His paternal grandfather was born a Swedish peasant with a different name—Ola Manson. He came to Minnesota from Sweden in 1860 and changed his name to August Lindbergh. Although stories vary on why August had to leave Sweden, Lynn and Dora Haines report that he had made powerful enemies because of his liberal political views. As a member of the Swedish parliament, he had championed legal protection for servants against their masters, abolition of the whipping post, and extended suffrage.[3] When he arrived in the Minnesota wilderness, he immediately became a leader of the community that was to spring up as Melrose. He helped establish a local school and served on the town council for many years.

Besides civic responsibility, August's reputation imparted to Charles the value of integrity and self-reliance. For example, on one occasion

August and C. A. walked to the county seat, some fifteen miles away, to pay off a debt. They had intended to use leftover money to rent lodging before returning the following morning. But when August paid the debt, he discovered he had miscalculated the interest and left himself too little money, even for food. Rather than depend on charity for the evening, he and C. A. walked the fifteen miles back home. C. A. repeated this account to young Charles, because he wanted the boy to accept the consequences of his errors and decisions.

A clearer example of August's physical courage and resolve was his loss of an arm when he fell into the blade of a logging saw in 1862. With his arm dangling by the tendons, August rode the ten miles to his home in a cart, waited for three days while a neighbor found the doctor in St. Cloud, and then underwent amputation without anesthesia. After recuperating for nearly two years he realized he must find some way to work on the farm. A special sling, balanced axe, and other custom-made tools were his solution to chopping wood and various heavy chores. This example of stoicism in the face of pain was a significant legacy. Although his grandfather died before he was born, Charles remembered August's unwillingness to succumb to self-pity and his mechanical resourcefulness as important lessons for his own life.

C. A. Lindbergh displayed many of the same family traits. He learned to shoot at nursery school age and became the family's sole supplier of meat and fish. He often went alone on errands to St. Cloud, a round trip of sixty miles, and was generally expected to be independent and self-sufficient. Although he attended school and eventually became a lawyer and congressman, he was an irregular student. Rote learning and school discipline didn't suit him. Yet, he read early and often. And he acquired August's tendency to radical views, which to C. A. meant an honest awareness of the plight of laborers or farmers and the excesses of the propertied classes. He established a law practice in Little Falls, Minnesota, and built a reputation on integrity and fair fees. Although he traded in farms and other real estate, he often loaned money to farmers so they wouldn't lose their farms to foreclosure. His political views and personal honesty made him a fine farmers' representative for the Sixth District in Minnesota. For a time, he resisted public life, but he was elected to the House of Representatives in 1907 and continued to serve until 1917.

Among the many characteristics Charles Lindbergh, Jr., absorbed from C. A., perhaps the most compelling were independence of mind and courage in adversity. C. A.'s philosophy of child rearing allowed Charles to grow up unbowed by adult views. He said: "Children manage much of the time to have their own way. That . . . is as it should be. The more child life is dominated, the easier adults are influenced. They become accustomed to having others direct them and do not think for themselves."[4] He taught Charles to solve his own problems and to maintain reasonable convictions, despite the "correctness" of opposing views.

His courage was especially evident during his race for governor of Minnesota in 1918, for this hard-fought primary campaign was marred by violence. At one point, C. A. came out of a meeting to find that a friend who had driven him had been dragged from the car and beaten by an armed mob. He fearlessly faced and spoke to them, causing them to fall back. Once he had gotten the friend into the car and started to drive away, however, the mob began shooting at them. When bullets actually hit the car, C. A. said to his friend: "We must not drive so fast. They will think we are afraid of them if we do."[5] Charles insisted he took little interest in politics or issues during his father's campaign, but he couldn't help but be impressed with the character and strength C. A. displayed until his death, of a cancerous brain tumor, in 1924.

From his mother's family, the Lodges and Lands, Lindbergh reaped equally important influences. Two stories of courage involved Grandmother Land and his mother, respectively. The first was of a lady left alone in a wilderness cabin, when a band of Indians came by and stole her husband's axe—an expensive item in those days. She put on her finest dress, followed them, and demanded that the thief return the stolen article. Apparently impressed by her fierce resolve, the Indian did so, and Grandmother Land returned with her prize to the cabin.[6] His mother demonstrated her will in a confrontation with the superintendent of Little Falls High School, where she was teaching chemistry in 1900. Forced to keep her chemistry laboratory in an ill-heated attic room at the school, she decided one winter day that it was simply too cold for her students. She carried the apparatus she was demonstrating down the stairs, only to be blocked by the superintendent. She put the apparatus at his feet, walked out of the school, and never taught there again.[7] Lindbergh was to remember these stories vividly throughout his life.

Perhaps more important to Lindbergh's development, however, was an abiding interest in science, which grew from his associations with Grandfather Land and other men of his mother's family. Dr. Charles Land was a dentist and inventor. He invented the first porcelain dentures, as well as many other gadgets and laboratory devices, and he was remarkably skillful with his hands. Charles often visited and played in his laboratory in Detroit, went on medical rounds with his Granduncle Lodge, and listened to discussions at the family table, which touted the logic of science over the myths of religion. As late as 1973, he was to recall these influences as one of two great callings in his life—the other being a deep love and appreciation for nature.

BOYHOOD AND EARLY VOCATION

These two impulses characterized Lindbergh's boyhood. He was born at the Land home in Detroit on February 4, 1902. But the family returned just six weeks later to Lindholm, C. A.'s 100-acre estate on the west bank of the Mississippi River. His earliest memories were of the large family home, with an upstairs view of the Mississippi, a beautiful grove of trees nearby, and several dogs for companionship. He also enjoyed the careful attention of his parents and two older half-sisters, Lillian and Eva, who were the offspring of C. A.'s earlier marriage. His years on the farm inculcated in him an enduring love of nature and a distaste for the bustle and cramped quarters of cities.

After the first few idyllic years, Charles's life changed because of two events. First, the family's large home burned down in late 1905. Although neighbors helped them save many of their possessions, all of his toys and belongings on the upper level were burned. The fire also forced them to move into a Minneapolis apartment for the winter and into a Little Falls hotel room while their new house was being built during the summer of 1906. Lindbergh considered apartment or hotel life dreary and boring. He spent most of his time watching people from a balcony overlooking the street. When he returned to the farm, he found the house much smaller and their finances more constrained. Fortunately, the new quarters did offer a view of woods and sky from a sleeping porch, on which Charles slept every night when he was in Little Falls.

A more important change occurred because of C. A.'s election to Congress for the Sixth District. From 1907 until 1917, Charles and his mother spent only summers at Little Falls. Each year, they traveled to Washington, D.C., so they could be near his father's offices. A picture taken in 1907 captures him at his father's side during the opening session of the House of Representatives, and several of his reminiscences show that he enjoyed the museums and attractions of the nation's capitol—if not its city lifestyle. Yet, the Lindberghs never lived together as a family after that year. Lillian and Eva went off to school, and his parents became estranged, though not formally separated. Mrs. Lindbergh traveled considerably with Charles, so they were not often actually with his father in the city.

Father and son did develop a good relationship, however. Every summer, C. A. returned to Little Falls to spend most of his time with Charles. Hunting, fishing, and camping were their favorite activities. Charles received his first rifle, a single-shot Stevens .22 caliber, from Grandfather Land when he was six years old. Although his father thought he might be a bit young for firearms, C.A. allowed him to carry it on their hunting trips and trusted him to follow safety rules laid down for him. From that year on, hunting was an important recreation for Lindbergh, though he eventually traded guns for a camera in the wilds of Africa and the Philippines.

Another activity that was to stay with him was swimming. As a youngster, he often rode on his father's back across the Mississippi, but as of the summer of 1910 he had not tried it on his own. When he accidentally waded into deep water, C. A. characteristically made no effort to save him. Charles recalls wondering whether he or his father was more surprised to see him suddenly swimming on his own. Soon afterward, he found he could swim with great endurance, and he prided himself on this stamina throughout his life. Even when he was in his sixties, he swam in every kind of weather, often breaking the ice in the cove at Darien, Connecticut, to exercise his powerful crawl.[8] Both the gun and swimming episodes illustrate the kind of upbringing Lindbergh experienced. His father believed that Charles must learn to rely upon himself and discover his abilities on his own. Perhaps these values were what led him to test himself against new frontiers in years to come.

Lindbergh's childhood years also marked a deep interest in things mechanical. Probably stemming from his visits to his grandfather's laboratory in Detroit, this interest developed into unusual skill at an early age. Lindbergh recalls being constantly busy at building things on the farm, often with his boyhood friends, Bill Thompson and Alex Johnson. Tree houses, an earthen cave and tunnel, a pair of wooden stilts, an ingenious board and pulley system for moving ice blocks from the river to the house—these were just a few of his accomplishments.[9] In 1913, at the age of eleven, he learned to drive the family car. From then on, he assumed more and more of their driving duties, eventually taking his mother on day trips and driving his father to campaign meetings throughout Minnesota. By 1916, he was able to squire his mother and Uncle Charles from Little Falls to California—a feat that required much mechanical ability to overcome poor roads, breakdowns, and meager supplies of parts.

Lindbergh's fascination with mechanics superseded his application in formal education. Until he entered army flight school in 1924, he was always an indifferent student. He found most high school subjects dry and useless, preferring to fill his notebooks with drawings of cars and airplanes rather than class notes. Meanwhile, he became increasingly skilled in taking apart and reassembling nearly every device he encountered.

By 1918, he was eager to take advantage of a special government program, which allowed students to gain a high school diploma by growing food to support the country's efforts in World War I. He took over Lindholm full-time, using his abilities in carpentry and mechanics to keep the farm running. He installed a water pumping system in the basement and experimented with making concrete fenceposts. Although these posts tended to crack apart after a time, he was successful with a concrete duck pond, christened "Moo Pond," which remains intact today. During this same time, Lindbergh discovered a way to wed his compulsion for tinkering to a fascination with speed and risk-taking. He bought a motorcycle and, according to neighbors, raced it at alarming speed down local roads and paths.

By 1920, Lindbergh had found farming enjoyable but not entirely satis-factory. He yearned to test himself in a less restrictive atmosphere—perhaps in flying on the Alaskan frontier. He had been enthralled with a barnstormer who came through Little Falls and with an air show he had seen at Fort Myer, Virginia. Flying seemed to combine all his interests—in mechanics, in physical risk as a proof of character, and in personal freedom. Moreover, he had learned that there was risk in everything one did, including farming. Although careful planning and safety-conscious-ness could decrease risk, one could never be entirely safe. He recalled that he had nearly been killed while plowing, when a plowshare released from his gangplow at the end of a row and whizzed by just six inches from his head. Reflecting on that episode, he decided that he should do something he truly wanted to do, despite the dangers it might involve.

When he informed his parents of his plan, however, they had other ideas. College-educated themselves, both parents believed Charles should have the benefits of a college education. As a dutiful son, he reluctantly agreed, hoping to study aeronautical engineering at Massa-chusetts Institute of Technology. But because his grades and high school background were mediocre, he had to settle for a mechanical engineering track—on a trial basis—at the University of Wisconsin. He matriculated fitfully for the next two years.

Lindbergh's successes came, as usual, outside the classroom. He spent much of his time tinkering with and racing his Excelsior motorcycle, occasionally testing himself on daredevil schemes to prove its perfor-mance. For a while, he was engrossed in building and sailing an ice-boat on a lake near the campus, but he eventually lost interest. Since he didn't date or take part in the social life of the university, the R.O.T.C. rifle and pistol teams were his only other important recreation. He liked most of the team members, as well as actual competitions, and he enjoyed some aspects of military organization. Among all these activities, however, he discovered little or no enthusiasm for coursework.

FLIGHT TRAINING AND BARNSTORMING

Eventually, in 1922, he began to investigate flying schools. With the help of a school friend, Delos Dudley, he obtained information on flying training from the Nebraska Aircraft Corporation and decided to quit school for good. After initial objections, Charles's parents sanctioned the plan, so he headed for Lincoln, Nebraska, at the end of March, never to return to formal university training.

When Charles arrived in Lincoln, he discovered one Lincoln Standard Turnabout airplane and a flight instructor, Ira Biffle, who had lost his taste for flying after a close friend died in a crash. Biffle often arrived at the airfield in the middle of the afternoon. If he found the slightest wind or hint of storm, he would call off Lindbergh's lesson for the day. As a result, Charles received just eight hours of flight instruction during his first six weeks in Lincoln. When the corporation's only plane had to be sold to obtain capital for additional construction, he still had not soloed. But he had experienced the joy of flying, and he knew he wanted to be a pilot. Because he had paid close attention to every detail of airplane construction and maintenance, he had also begun to acquire the practical knowledge of design that he had missed by not completing college.

Despite the experience he had gained, however, Lindbergh knew that he needed much more training. In May, he talked a pilot named Erold Bahl into taking him as a helper on a month-long barnstorming tour of the western states. Although he had spent a good bit of his savings on flying lessons, he even offered to pay his own expenses on the tour. At first, he cleaned Bahl's plane, pulled the propeller to help start it, and hawked passengers from small towns—at five dollars a ride. After a few days, he convinced Bahl that they would draw better crowds if he did some wingwalking. Despite a childhood fear of falling, which had often caused him nightmares, he stepped out onto the wing and stood there while Bahl circled over the towns along their route. Lindbergh downplayed the danger involved, pointing out that he was secured to the wing by cables, which were invisible to the crowds below. Still, it demonstrated his willingness to take reasonable risks, if some benefit were to be gained from them.

When the tour ended in June, Lindbergh was no closer to soloing and much shorter on ready cash. He returned to Lincoln to work in the Nebraska Aircraft Corporation's factory for fifteen dollars a week. At least this job gave him more training in aircraft construction, and because he lived at the airfield, it kept him near planes and pilots. Within a few days, it also gave him a chance to conquer his fear of falling by taking his first parachute jump.

When a parachute maker, Charles Hardin, came to Lincoln to demonstrate his wares, Lindbergh decided that he must jump. He remembered later that he had a feeling of "anticipation mixed with dread, of confidence restrained by caution, of courage salted through with fear." He knew that he had neither pay nor acclaim nor scientific observation to gain by jumping, but he was lured by the adventure of air and sky, "where man is more than man, and existence both supreme and valueless at the same instant."[10] After a bit of instruction, he went up to 1800 feet, crawled out to the end of the wing with his double parachute in a canvas bag, and leaped off into space to try a "double jump." The first chute caught correctly and slowed his descent, then drifted away as the second chute began to emerge from the bag. But Hardin had tied the chutes together with bad string, so the first one broke loose too soon. Lindbergh rushed toward the earth as the second chute remained bunched near his back. Finally it caught the air and billowed, just a few hundred feet from the ground, and he landed hard but unhurt. He had tested himself and emerged victorious, never again to be plagued by his childhood nightmares of falling.

Soon after Charles arrived back in Lincoln, he met a veteran pilot, H. J. "Shorty" Lynch, who taught him more flying in his off hours. By July, Lindbergh was ready to solo, but Lynch was on his way to a barnstorming tour through Kansas and neighboring states, so he asked Charles along as wingwalker and parachutist. It was an opportunity he couldn't pass up. From July to October he traveled with Lynch through four states, billed as DAREDEVIL LINDBERGH on the flyers that preceded them. When money and crowds wore thin in October, he returned to Lincoln for his motorcycle and rode it to Detroit to see his mother. After a few weeks, he joined his father for the winter in Little Falls and Minneapolis.

The time with his parents was pleasant, but he kept thinking that he still hadn't become a flyer in his own right. He heard that surplus Curtiss "Jennies" were for sale at Souther Field, Georgia. Perhaps buying his own plane would solve the trouble he had had finding people to teach him to fly. He talked his father into cosigning a loan for him and left for Georgia in April with cash and checks in hand. Once he had chosen a Jenny and paid for it, he faced the problem of flying it away. Minimal instruction without soloing hadn't prepared him for his first lurching trip off the runway . . . and quickly back onto it again. Fortunately, a pilot named Henderson came to his aid. After several flights, he finally soloed and landed at sunset.

Lindbergh spent another week practicing before taking off toward Montgomery, Alabama, and Mississippi. He began offering rides to townspeople along the way. Although business was spotty, he made $250 in a day at Maben, Mississippi. Unfortunately, he also cracked up his plane in a hidden ditch northwest of Meridian, ruining one of his two propellers and causing a week's delay for parts. Nothing dampened his enthusiasm for flying, however. In the sky he felt almost god-like, exhilarated by the rush of wind and his view of the world below. To his delight, his parents shared his enjoyment. When he returned to Minnesota to show them his new skill, C. A. asked Charles to pilot him on a campaign tour, and his mother liked flying so much that she accompanied him on a ten-day barnstorming tour in July. All seemed right in the world, for he was finally "one of them"—slipping the bonds of earth for the freedom of the skies.

As the year wore on, however, Lindbergh found that freedom did not necessarily guarantee him a living. Passengers were harder to come by, and the skies were growing thicker with barnstormers seeking the same markets. At the end of the summer, Charles found himself barely meeting expenses. Although he had become a good pilot, he also knew he could not progress in the art of flying unless he received more training in newer planes. That training was available only through the Army Air Corps. Balancing his own freedom against a practical need for training and a declining barnstorming market, he decided to join—if he could pass the entrance examination. After attending the air races at Lambert Field in St. Louis during the fall of 1923, he sold his Jenny and traveled to Chanute Field, Illinois, to take the examination in January 1924. In February, he received notice that he had passed the test and must report for training by March 19 at Brooks Field, in San Antonio, Texas. Thus, he was to begin a more rigorous phase in his drive to become a great pilot.

Lindbergh had a month of adventures before reporting. He had met Leon Klink at Lambert Field and had begun instructing him in flying his "Canuck" airplane. In fact, they had barnstormed through several southern states during January, before Lindbergh obtained his acceptance notice in Pensacola, Florida. One day, they were flying near Pensacola, when the Canuck's engine cut out, and they crashed into a field. The results were a crushed landing gear, splintered propeller, and broken spar on the left wing, but no personal injuries.

By February 20, they had repaired the plane and were ready to take Klink to California, where Lindbergh intended to catch a train back to Brooks Field. As a lark, he dropped the plane down into a town square at Camp Wood, Texas. Next day, the wind had shifted, forcing them to take off down the main street, with one foot of clearance for each wingtip. Lindbergh nearly made it, but one wing caught a telephone pole and veered the plane through a hardware store window. The store owner refused payment for damages, claiming the publicity would more than pay for the loss of his store front. But they had to delay several days for repairs. When they finally did get away, they tore a wing upon landing that same evening.

ARMY AND AIRMAIL PILOT

All these problems used too much time to reach California, so Klink took a train the rest of the way, promising to return for his plane and more lessons in a few weeks. Meanwhile, Lindbergh flew his battered craft into Brooks Field. When an army flight sergeant unceremoniously ordered him to get his piece of junk off the field, he got his first taste of army life. He parked the plane at nearby Stinson Field and returned to enlist on March 19—one of 104 beginning aviation cadets.

Flight training proved to be especially difficult at first. Lindbergh had to adjust to the left-hand throttles and greater power of army Jennies, as well as to the rigorous requirements of ground school. He flew with the army each morning, attended ground school in the afternoon, continued to instruct Klink at nearby Stinson Field in the evening, and studied at night. His first examination grade was a 72 percent—barely passing. For the first time in his life, he became concerned about academic study. He wanted to graduate.

By June 1924 almost half of Lindbergh's class had washed out, but his grades were up to 90 percent, and he was second among his remaining classmates. By September, only thirty-three people were left of the original 104. With the others, Charles moved to Kelly Field for the second six months of training in more powerful De Havillands—the plane he had joined the army to fly. The precise training and rigorous procedures made him into the pilot he had wanted to become. After several months of work in formation flying, bombing, strafing, gunnery practice, and reconnaissance, he moved into pursuit—the most difficult and most heralded form of army flying—just six weeks before graduation. When he graduated in March 1925 and was commissioned a Second Lieutenant in the Army Air Service Reserve, he was first in the class of eighteen men remaining in the program.

It would be a mistake, however, to think that Lindbergh was all study and seriousness. His penchant for practical jokes found a particularly ripe field within the regimentation of army life. He described with relish such tricks as piling an absent recruit's clothes in the middle of the barracks, placing the drill sergeant's cot on top of a building, putting a hose with running water into someone's bed, filling a sleeper's open mouth with shaving cream, and so on. This sort of trickery became a trademark throughout his life, even in the august company of European and New England society.

Another trademark was his continuing flirtation with adventure and danger. Just a few days before graduation from flight school, he risked being washed out by "dogfighting" another De Havilland in extremely poor visibility conditions. After several loops and exhilarating turns and dives, he thought he saw a flight instructor in the other plane. If the instructor had reported him, he would have been finished. Fortunately, he was not identified to the school commandant, so he escaped unscathed.

Soon afterward, though, he encountered a problem from which he could not escape. Just nine days before graduation, he was involved in an in-flight accident near Galveston, Texas. During mock-attack maneuvers with fellow cadet Phil Love and a Lt. McAllister, Lindbergh climbed into McAllister and locked wings with his SE-5 trainer. The planes began to spin as both men parachuted away from them. Suddenly, Lindbergh looked up to see the spinning ships coming directly at him, as he floated helplessly in the harness. Remarkably, the planes took a turn away from him at just the right moment, and they missed him by 200 or 300 feet. He landed safely in a plowed field, having lost only his goggles, vest-pocket camera, and the rip cord of the parachute.[11] For this escapade, he and

McAllister became members twelve and thirteen of the Caterpillar Club—men who had to parachute from planes to save their lives. As a premonition of the luck that seemed to accompany Lindbergh's exploits, it is worth noting that his class was the first to be issued parachutes. One year earlier, he would have died.

When Lindbergh was commissioned in March, the army didn't need pilots, so he was released to find civilian employment. In St. Louis, he was offered the job of chief pilot for the Robertson Aircraft Corporation, a company that was bidding on government contracts to fly the airmail from St. Louis to Chicago. While waiting to see if Robertson was awarded the contract, he taught local people to fly and tested new planes at Lambert Field. In May 1925 he had yet another brush with death. During testing of a plane built by an engineer at Lambert, he went into a left spin and finally had to jump just 350 feet above the ground. The chute opened, but the plane spun to within less than 100 feet from him. Charles later observed that one couldn't come closer to death than that, and if he were to get a glimpse of the beyond, this would have been the occasion for it.[12] But the plane missed him, and he landed safely.

Lindbergh was still waiting for the airmail contract in August, when the Mil-Hi Airways and Flying Circus, of Denver, offered him a pilot's job. He took the $400 per month position, because he thought it would allow him to test his plane in mountains and canyons, thus making him aware of the effects of downdrafts, currents, and turbulence on aircraft. Many times, he flew late into the night and landed in fields, with only the beam of a flashlight to guide him safely to the ground. Yet, he didn't regret any of these hair-raising experiences. The risks involved, he felt, were justified by his sheer love of the life he led.

A few months later, he was back in St. Louis, laying out the mail run for Robertson. He hired ex-army buddies Phil Love and Thomas Nelson to help him. By connecting daily with mail runs from Chicago to the east coast, the airmail could beat overland service by one full day. With no lights on airfields and poor navigation equipment and weather information, this flying was anything but routine. Moreover, Robertson was a shoestring operation, as so many companies were in the early days of flying. Lindbergh employed farmers and others along the route to keep small signal lights operating. Local service people brought gasoline to the fields in trucks. For illumination in night landings, the pilots used parachute flares, but Robertson equipped them with only one flare per plane.

On one occasion, Charles had to jump from his plane when it ran out of gas in a heavy fog near Chicago. He touched down in a cornfield and was found by a startled farmer. The farmer drove him into a small town, where he could put the mail bags on the train to the city, thus fulfilling their delivery contract. Despite these problems, though, Lindbergh established a system that flew five round-trips each week, with 99 percent efficiency, throughout 1926 and early 1927.

NEW YORK TO PARIS

On one of his mail runs from Peoria to Chicago, Lindbergh mused about the possibilities of long-distance flight, especially with the recently developed Wright-Bellanca monoplane and Wright "Whirlwind" engine. He thought that such a plane, loaded with gasoline, could "break the world's endurance record, and the transcontinental, and set a dozen marks for range and speed and weight." Possibly, he could even fly nonstop between New York and Paris.[13] From the time this thought entered his startled mind, he started planning a transatlantic flight.

The New York to Paris idea wasn't entirely accidental. Lindbergh knew that Raymond Orteig, a New York hotel owner born in France, had offered a prize of $25,000 for a nonstop flight in either direction between the two cities. He also must have been aware that others intended to claim the prize in the spring of 1927. His competition would include the famous Arctic explorer, Commander Richard Byrd, navy fliers Noel Davis and Stanton Wooster, Clarence Chamberlin, and the French pilots, Charles Nungesser and François Coli. But he intended to make the flight alone. He had faced miserable weather and fog, as well as lengthy periods without sleep, so he believed he was up to the Atlantic challenge. All he needed was the financial backing to secure a properly equipped plane, and he would do the rest.

From September 1926 to February 1927, frustrations mounted. After careful planning and several appeals, he was able to obtain backing from a group of St. Louis businessmen, who were also interested in flight. Earl Thompson, Harold Bixby, and Harry Knight helped him put together enough money to purchase a Wright-Bellanca. When he traveled to the factory in November, however, he was refused the sale. The plane went instead to Charles Levine, of the Columbia Aircraft Corporation, because Levine's organization seemed more likely to accomplish the flight. Other airplane builders turned him down as well, unimpressed by what appeared to be a foolhardy attempt at a solo crossing.

Finally, on February 3, Lindbergh wired Ryan Airlines of California and received a bid the next day. Ryan offered to build the plane for $6,000 plus the cost of a Wright engine and to deliver it in three months. Unfortunately, Lindbergh needed it in two months in order to beat his competition. He traveled to San Diego to see the plant, and the facilities were hardly impressive. But the sincerity of Ryan's president, B. F. Mahoney, and of chief engineer Donald Hall were compelling. Without guaranteeing the design, Mahoney convinced Lindbergh to let them try to meet his deadline.

Hall and Lindbergh began working together on the Ryan NY-P monoplane, which was to become the famous *Spirit of St. Louis*. The design itself was years ahead of its time. A wide wingspan, narrow fuselage, and enlarged fuel tanks were built solely for long-distance flight. Although the plane tended to be unstable, requiring constant attention from the pilot to keep it at level flight, the resulting performance gave it a higher airspeed—much like today's jet fighters. Every other design feature, as well as Lindbergh's decisions on what to take with him, depended on reducing weight and increasing safety. Lindbergh traded an unreliable radio for ninety pounds of gas. He removed the sextant because he wouldn't be able to work it during flight, thus saving more weight. He even ripped spare pages from his notebook and cut holes in his navigation charts for areas he didn't expect to fly over. And he studied charts and weather information day after day. No flight was more meticulously planned.

By May, the plane and all flight testing were finished. As several of Lindbergh's rivals met with crashes and other problems, the press began taking his plans seriously. When Nungesser and Coli took off from Le Bourget Field in Paris and then disappeared over the Atlantic, he decided to move as quickly as possible to New York and to go at the first sign of clearing weather. On May 10, he set a new world speed record for air travel on a 1,600-mile nonstop flight from San Diego to St. Louis. There, his backers encouraged him to go on, so he completed the cross-country trip, again in record time. The two legs added together set a new transcontinental speed record, thus giving Lindbergh one of the accomplishments he had only imagined the previous year.

Lindbergh's mounting reputation as a pilot was a mixed blessing. On one hand, he received respect from the Wright organization, who sent an ace mechanic to help him prepare for the flight. Many other suppliers jumped on the bandwagon, offering gas, oil, and equipment at no cost. On the other, he was plagued by the press and the attention of curiosity seekers. Many newspaper reports emphasized the dangers of the Atlantic flight. Others began tagging him with nicknames like "Lucky Lindy" and trying to obtain information on his personal life. Eventually, he met people like Harry Bruno and Dick Blythe, who were able to handle the press for him and keep him somewhat insulated from the public.

As Lindbergh waited tensely for the weather to clear over the ocean, he began to make contacts that would launch his career as a commercial aviator after the famous flight. Harry Guggenheim, a financier of aviation under the Daniel Guggenheim Fund, frankly thought he was doomed, but he told him to look him up when he returned to the United States. A promotional tour for aviation would be a good bet with a famous flier at its forefront. Some of New York's finest reporters, people Lindbergh was to respect throughout his life, came to interview him. Lauren D. Lyman of the *Times* and C. B. Allen of the *Post* were among them. Most important to the flier himself, however, were the famous designers and pilots, who now treated him as an equal.

Although Charles enjoyed these associations, he chafed at the delays. On the night before his flight, a heavy rainstorm blanketed the East Coast and the Atlantic. He had gone to see a new Broadway review, when he got a forecast for unexpected clearing skies over the ocean, possibly enough to allow him to take off in the morning. He went back to his hotel and tried to sleep, but couldn't. He rose before dawn and went to the airfield, which was muddy and shrouded in a continuous drizzle. With his engine turning thirty revolutions low and the wind shifting to his tail, he decided to go. He cleared the telephone wires at the end of the runway by just twenty feet and turned toward Nova Scotia, Ireland, and Paris. Presently the rain stopped, the mist and clouds began to clear away, and a tailwind was blowing. Lindbergh's historic flight had begun.

The hours that followed were a period of magnificent human endurance. Through storms, fog, ice clouds, and most of all, an overpowering need for sleep, Lindbergh endured. Despite times when he literally punched himself in the face to keep awake, times when ghostly presences appeared to fill his cockpit and he drifted in a state between life and death, he kept reminding himself that the only alternative to staying awake was "death and failure, death and failure." Almost miraculously, he finally arrived at the coast of Ireland just three miles off course. Fatigued as he was, he spurned its safety for another six hours of flight to Paris. He ate his first food in thirty-five hours at the coast of France, then flew directly into Le Bourget, touching down in the darkness after thirty-three hours, thirty minutes and 3,614 miles in the air.

Although Charles had prepared for every conceivable problem on the flight itself, nothing could have prepared him for the reception that followed. Thousands of French people had gathered at Le Bourget to welcome him. He was hoisted on their shoulders and jostled through the air. Finally, two French fliers, Detroyat and Delage, spirited him away from the crowd and took him to the safety of a hangar. There, he met Ambassador Myron Herrick and asked that his plane be brought inside, before souvenir seekers tore it to shreds. They secured the much-damaged plane but lost his carefully prepared log of the flight, which remains missing today.

Ambassador Herrick managed to get Lindbergh back to the American embassy in Paris, so the flier could tell his exclusive story to J. Carlisle MacDonald, of the *New York Times*. But MacDonald soon recognized that the story was too big to hold under one banner. Once he released it and Charles to other newspapers, the hero-making press swung into action throughout the world, becoming less and less accurate as the distance from the source increased. All emphasized his boyish grin, good looks, modesty, and honest American character.

Then, too, Charles added to their impressions by instinctively making the right gestures. He wired congratulations to all who had helped him get to Paris, made a transatlantic call to his mother, and visited the mother of Nungesser, one of the Frenchmen who had died in an attempt to fly from Paris to New York. He won the hearts of the French people when he told her that Nungesser and Coli had tried a more difficult task— against headwinds and a storm front. He appeared "unspoiled" by success.

Over the next two months, Lindbergh experienced an overwhelming outpouring of public recognition. He was mobbed on goodwill trips to Belgium and London, where he had audiences with royalty. President Calvin Coolidge sent the cruiser *Memphis*, flagship of the U.S. European fleet, to bring him home from England. When he arrived in June, the president made him a colonel in the Army Air Corps Reserves and bestowed upon him the first Distinguished Flying Cross. The capstone of these celebrations was a tickertape parade in New York City, arranged by Mayor Jimmy Walker. Crowds there were estimated at 4 million, and Lindbergh received the city's Medal of Valor, as well as the New York State Medal of Honor from Governor Alfred E. Smith. Finally, more than 2 million people sent letters of congratulations—5,000 of which also contained commemorative poems—and hundreds of streets, mountains, towns, and babies were named after him.[14]

During the next several weeks, Charles had to thread a course between offers totaling $5 million for personal appearances, speaking tours, and films. He rejected everyone who wanted to exploit his fame, deciding instead to tell his own story and to work for the benefit of commercial aviation. Although he received 15,000 presents from sixty-nine countries —worth more than $2 million, he signed nearly all of them over to the Missouri Historical Society. He also returned a large sum of money to donors, asking them to use the money for charities or to develop aviation. These actions added to the world's image of him as a thoroughly uncorruptible young man.

Yet, he benefitted greatly from the historic flight. His writing and interviews for the *New York Times* netted him $65,000. *We*, the brief account of his early life and transatlantic junket, written in three weeks at Harry Guggenheim's home in Long Island, brought total royalties of $200,000. And a forty-eight-state tour to promote commercial aviation, sponsored by the Daniel Guggenheim Fund, paid him $50,000 between July and October of 1927.

COMMERCIAL FLIGHTS AND OTHER INTERESTS

A number of Lindbergh's lifelong predilections emerged during this tour. He insisted on timely arrivals and departures, careful plotting and use of maps, flying always on straight lines between points, and absolute safety for bystanders at towns and airports. He knew he must show the world that commercial aviation was reliable and safe, if it was to progress. As Charles traveled under constant public scrutiny, he also began to reveal his almost schizophrenic private and public personalities. Walter Ross notes in *The Last Hero* that Charles was the warm, joking, easygoing "Slim" with companions Donald Keyhoe and Phil Love. He enjoyed meeting anyone he had known before Paris, especially the barnstormers and test pilots whom he had considered brothers of the sky. But he became the "serious Colonel of public events" as soon as the public intruded.[15]

As Leonard Mosley points out in his biography of Lindbergh, Charles was uncomfortable around women his own age, as well. With young men he was "like a cowboy in a bunkhouse, full of tricks and practical jokes, always ready for a jape." But with girls, he was shy, tongue-tied, or disdainful.[16] In fairness to Lindbergh, however, the general acclaim, often silly attentions of women, and attempted exploitation of his fame had taken a toll on his private life. The newspapers were less interested in the purpose of his flying tour than in his private affiliations or romances, so he also became increasingly sour on the press.

Despite his aversion to reporters, Lindbergh was grateful for their influence on aviation. His well-reported tour of eighty-two cities spurred tremendous interest in the airplane, which led in turn to hundreds of improvements in airfields—especially lighting and marking of roofs as navigational aids—and a huge increase in the volume of airmail moving across the country.

Soon after his return to Mitchell Field, New York, he seized upon this public recognition by planning a goodwill tour of Latin America, which would become a major airmail customer during the 1920s. The ambassador to Mexico, Dwight Morrow, wanted to promote diplomatic and commercial ties with our southern neighbors, so he was pleased to use Lindbergh's popularity for the purpose.

Lindbergh took off for Mexico City in December of 1927, arriving to a 150,000-strong reception headed by the Mexican president. There he was a guest of the Morrow family, including his future wife, Anne Spencer Morrow, the shy, sensitive, blue-eyed daughter of the ambassador. Although he had met Anne briefly in New York, this Christmas stay gave them a chance to become better acquainted. Unquestionably, Anne was taken by what she described as his "small-boy-hands-in-pockets looking-straight-at-you attitude." In *Bring Me a Unicorn*, her diary of the period, she calls Charles "great"—with tremendous unconscious power over people, and she notes his dignity, youth, and clean-cut freshness.[17] Although Charles appeared indifferent to her, their relationship would grow into marriage by May of 1929.

For the next several months, though, Charles had other obligations. He flew 9,000 miles to seventeen Latin American countries, finishing with a fifteen and a half hour flight from Havana to St. Louis. Besides promoting good will between the countries and the United States, he also did some air sampling experiments and a bit of aerial surveying of archeological ruins, thus combining his interests in flying and science. In March of 1928, he received the Congressional Medal of Honor at the White House, and in April, he dedicated the *Spirit of St. Louis* to the Smithsonian Institution for permanent display. The following month, he found his niche as a technical consultant to Transcontinental Air Transport (TAT) and Pan American Airways (Pan Am), both destined to become modern giants in air transport. It was the perfect position for him. As a consultant, he could be in the vanguard of aviation development without being bound to a salaried, nine to five job. Above all, he could plan and fly new routes, thus turning what he enjoyed most into good business for himself and his St. Louis partners.

Fortunately, he was able to work for two airlines with no conflict of interests. TAT developed a transcontinental route, combining railroad and air links from New York to California. Called "The Lindbergh Line" in advertisements, this service could move passengers coast-to-coast in forty-eight hours—a savings of twenty-four hours over the railroad alone. Pan Am, on the other hand, opened up mail and passenger service to Central and South America from Miami. Plans called for expanding into other foreign countries but not flying within the United States. Charles became involved in every major decision concerning the growth of both companies, and his technical demands spurred rapid development in the airplane industry.

Having established himself in business, Charles was prepared for his future, which soon involved Anne Morrow. He began to see Anne in New York, sometimes taking her for flying lessons at a local airfield. They became secretly engaged, spent several weeks together at Mexico City and Cuernavaca, and eventually had their formal engagement announced in February 1929. They were married that May, at the Morrow home in Englewood, New Jersey.

Because Charles was destined to lead a public life, Anne had much adjusting to do, including learning how to deal with the constant attentions of the press. Her lessons began on her wedding day. Although they managed to disguise themselves after the ceremony and escape the press temporarily, reporters eventually caught up with them at the harbor. Some particularly enterprising newsmen rented a boat and followed the Lindberghs onto the bay, where the newlyweds intended to take a honeymoon cruise. After hours of circling and rocking the Lindberghs' craft, they finally gave up and left them alone. This experience was to begin a long war between the Lindberghs and the press. Anne and Charles often wore disguises and kept family news quiet, tending to make themselves an "item" by their secretiveness.

Fortunately, Anne's spirit and determination were usually equal to the task, for Lindbergh's active life style kept him constantly on the move. Soon after they were wed, they went to California to obtain a new monoplane from Lockheed. Lindbergh lived at the plant while it was being built in Burbank, so he could participate in its initial testing. By the time the monoplane, christened *Sirius*, was ready to fly to New York in April 1930, Anne was in her seventh month of pregnancy. Although they set a new speed record—seven hours faster than Lindbergh had traveled in the *Spirit* just three years earlier—Anne was very ill for four of the fourteen hours in the air. She asked Charles to dismiss the press in New York, because she thought her illness might harm his reputation for safe flight. His curt dismissal fueled existing animosities, and late-stayers made a special point of reporting Anne's poor condition as she was carried from the plane.

While living in California, Lindbergh had become interested in another form of air travel—rocketry. He thought of using rocket-powered thrust as a booster to conventional planes in case of engine failure. When he contacted Vought Corporation engineers about the concept, they referred him to Dr. Robert Goddard, who has since become known as the father of modern rocketry. His meeting with Goddard marked the beginning of a sixteen-year association between the two men, as well as the first serious funding of Goddard's projects.

Despite many failures, which often led Goddard to despair, Lindbergh obtained nearly a quarter of a million dollars from the Guggenheim Foundation to finance the rocket scientist's experiments and laboratory at Roswell, New Mexico. He wrote a public letter of appreciation concerning Goddard's work and its future in 1938, predicting that rockets would become important to astronomy, meteorology, and terrestrial magnetism, as well as to military applications and interstellar flight. Eventually, he was vindicated by several startling advances. A liquid-fuel rocket that Goddard shot 9,000 feet into the air in 1941 had nearly all the features later incorporated into the German V-2. In fact, Wernher von Braun, the famous German scientist, has said that "every liquid-fuel rocket that flies is a Goddard rocket."[18] Lindbergh's vision and practical determination combined to help make Goddard's dream a reality.

Soon after Lindbergh acquired the Guggenheim grant for Robert Goddard in the spring of 1930, he turned his attention to becoming a father for the first time. On June 22 Charles Augustus Lindbergh, Jr., was born at the Morrow residence. To provide him and Anne a real home, Charles purchased 400 acres of land near Hopewell, New Jersey, and began putting up a house, meantime renting a place near Princeton. Lindbergh was not a doting father, for he was too much a product of his own stoical upbringing, but he did spend time with baby Charles and admired the child's good health.

Family responsibilities did not slow down the Lindberghs' hectic pace, however. They were able to leave the baby with Mrs. Morrow and a nurse, sequestered within the safety of the Morrows' walls at Englewood. By fall, they were planning a surveying flight to the Orient over the northern route—through Canada, the Kamchatka Peninsula, and south to Japan and China. This arduous trip required Anne to be crew rather than mere passenger. Both Charles and Anne needed third-class radio operator licenses, which demanded study of physics, electronics, and navigation. Careful navigating and advance shipments of supplies and equipment to points along the route were necessities for survival. Thus, nights of detailed planning slipped into months, as they aimed for takeoff in July of the following year.

In the midst of the Lindberghs' preoccupations, tragedy came to Anne's family. Her older sister, Elisabeth, revealed a terminal heart condition, with no hope of a life-saving operation. Charles wanted to find out why no one could operate to repair the heart. He was referred to Dr. Alexis Carrel, a Nobel Laureate for his techniques of suturing blood vessels during operations and for transplantation of organs, and he met the famous man at the Rockefeller Institute in November 1930. Unfortunately, Carrel could not help Elisabeth, for no means had yet been invented to keep organs alive outside the body while repairs were made. Anne's sister died within months of their meeting.

Lindbergh's discovery of Dr. Carrel had a strong effect on him, nevertheless. From Carrel's description of the mechanical apparatus needed for Elisabeth's operation, Charles was to invent a glass perfusion pump that would make such operations possible in the future. He set to work immediately, but he had to endure four years of trial and error—off and on—before he finally solved the problem. Meanwhile, he developed a method of washing blood corpuscles for Carrel's experiments and invented a quick way of separating serum from whole blood by means of a centrifuge.[19] Between flying trips with Anne, Charles became thoroughly engrossed in and made significant contributions to medical technology.

Lindbergh's first priority continued to be flying, however, because he hoped his pioneering survey trips would help open up the world to intercontinental air travel and, therefore, to international communication. Anne pioneered as well, for she was the first woman in America to hold a radio operator's license. In fact, she was depressed by the questions of friends and reporters on domestic issues and feminine concerns, such as the color and type of dresses she was taking along on their trip to the Orient. Allowed but one pair of shoes and only eighteen pounds of luggage, she considered herself crew, and that is precisely what Charles expected.[20] Her accounts of forced landings near Nome, Alaska, and between Kamchatka and Japan left no doubt that she was often afraid during the fog-bound trips, but she kept tenaciously to her radio post while Lindbergh battled the elements.

By September 1931 they were in China's Hingwa province, having offered their plane to fly relief supplies and food to famine and flood victims. In one instance the hungry Chinese stormed the plane, and Charles had to fire his revolver in the air to frighten them back just long enough to taxi away. Finally, the *Sirius* was damaged and sunk by junks in Hankow harbor. Although a British aircraft carrier salvaged the craft, it was not immediately repairable. At the same time, the Lindberghs received word that Anne's father had died of a stroke, so they shipped their plane to California for repairs and booked passage for a return cruise to the States. The historic trip was over, and an airline route that is still flown today was discovered and charted.

TRAGEDY AND TRIUMPH

After returning home, the Lindberghs spent much time with Mrs. Morrow to console her and keep her active with baby Charles. By February, their home near Hopewell was finished, so they began to spend weekends there. They changed their routine on February 29, because Anne and Charles, Jr., had colds, so they were all at Hopewell on the evening of March 1—a Tuesday. It was to become a devastating change. Charles heard a sound like orange crate slats breaking at 9:00 P.M., but because it was a windy night, he thought little of it. Sadly, when the boy's nurse went to get him for a feeding at 10:00, she found him missing. A kidnap note was in an envelope propped on a radiator, and muddy footprints were on the floor. One of the most infamous kidnapping cases in America had begun.

Charles went out with his rifle to check the grounds while his butler called the local police. He touched nothing, knowing that the police would want everything undisturbed. When the New Jersey state police arrived, they opened the ransom envelope and discovered a semi-literate note asking for $50,000 in various denominations and warning against making the kidnapping public or notifying the police. The kidnappers promised the child was "in gut care" and signed the note with two intersecting red circles, filled in with blue at the intersection and punched with square holes at the centers. This distinctive logo was to authenticate subsequent notes.[21] On the ground below Charles, Jr.'s, window, the police found a wooden ladder made of three pieces joined by dowels, with one rung broken. A carpenter's chisel was also lying nearby, and a number of footprints were discovered in the soft earth. These were the meager clues with which state police began their investigation.

In the days and months following the kidnapping, Charles and Anne lived through many false hopes and alarms, as well as bizarre offers of help from people as diverse as a former Justice Department agent and ex-convict, Gaston Means; a retired schoolteacher, Dr. John F. (Jafsie) Condon; and even the imprisoned gangster, Al Capone. Many people were trying to parlay the kidnapping into personal gain. For example, Means claimed he knew the kidnapper to be a fellow convict from the Atlanta penitentiary. He promised to have the baby delivered for $100,000. Evalyn Walsh McLean, the owner of the Hope diamond, had offered to pay the ransom for the Lindberghs, so she gave Means the money—never to see it or the baby again. Capone intended to trade his release from jail in Chicago for information leading to Charles, Jr.'s, discovery. Unfortunately, his contacts did not know anything about the baby, so his offer was a hollow one. Meanwhile, each false alarm made the Lindberghs more frantic.

Of all the people who offered aid, Dr. John Condon appeared to be most authentic. He wrote a letter to the *Bronx Home News* offering his own savings and the ransom money in exchange for the baby. He promised the kidnappers secrecy and said he would go anywhere to act as a go-between. Late on the night of March 9, he got a written reply to his advertisement, asking him to acquire $70,000 and place an ad in the paper saying "money is ready" when he got it. Lindbergh authorized Condon's actions, which eventually brought him face-to-face with a man who called himself John and who exhibited the same Germanic accent, grammar, misspellings, and handwriting as in the kidnap note.

The fateful meeting came the night of April 2, 1932, at St. Raymond's Cemetery. Lindbergh and Condon drove to a nearby street, where Charles remained parked within hearing distance of the cemetery. In fact, Lindbergh clearly heard a man inside yell "Hey, Doctor" to attract Condon's attention. Condon went on to meet "John" and bargained to give him $50,000 in return for a memo of the baby's whereabouts. Both men were ecstatic when they thought they had an authentic note referring them to the "Boad Nelly . . . between Horseneck Beach and Gay Head near Elizabeth Island." But a thorough search of the area turned up no boat and no Charles, Jr.

While these events were unfolding, John Hughes Curtis, a Virginia boatbuilder, claimed that he had contacted a Scandinavian who was holding the Lindbergh baby on a schooner near Cape May, New Jersey. He convinced Lindbergh to join him in searching the waters around Cape May for nearly three weeks during April and May. Charles was still looking when he got word on May 12 that the baby had been found dead, in a shallow grave about a mile from the Lindbergh house. The autopsy showed a fractured skull, which police speculated had occurred in a fall from the ladder on the night of the kidnapping. The child's nurse, Betty Gow, identified him that day, but Lindbergh went to view the remains on May 13, so he would have no more doubts about the child's death. He counted teeth, saw a foot with turned in toes like Charles, Jr.'s, said it was his baby, and ordered the remains cremated. Their uncertainty had ended. All that remained was to discover and punish the person who had committed the murder. But that was to take another four years.

In the interim, the Lindberghs somehow had to return to a normal life. They could not go back to Hopewell, so they donated it to a nonprofit organization to "provide for the welfare of children . . . without discrimination in regard to race or creed." Called High Fields, it became a well-known home for boys.[22] Once removed from the scene of her heartache, Anne was able to concentrate on her pregnancy, which resulted in the birth of her second son, Jon, on August 16, 1932. Charles immediately issued a statement to the press, asking the public to allow his son to grow up normally. His plea fell on deaf ears. Letters threatened Jon's life, and reporters pressed to take his picture and write stories about the Lindbergh family. Finally, Charles and Anne placed Jon under guard at Englewood and bought a watch dog to protect him, so they could resume their flying and other activities.

Fortunately, an expedition was looming to take their minds from their sorrow. Juan Trippe of Pan Am wanted them to fly and map Atlantic routes in the north and south, with a view toward major expansion of Pan Am's commitments overseas. They prepared during the fall and spring, then took off for Greenland and Copenhagen in July 1933. Charles mapped terrain and took meteorological readings enroute, mailing reports back to Trippe as they went. He recommended a summer schedule for the Greenland-Iceland route, with experimental flying during the rest of the year by people committed to the north country's future.[23] His weather information and maps were invaluable to further commercial flying in the Arctic.

After traveling for several months in Europe, they arrived at Santiago in the Cape Verde Islands, poised for a 1600-mile flight across the Atlantic from British Gambia to Natal, Brazil. Anne later wrote of this trip in *Listen! The Wind*, pointing out that there were no airfields, no advance information about landing conditions, and no assurance that they could reach alternate destinations. Safety lay "not in dogmatic formulas of performance and structure, but in the proper balance of constantly changing factors," which only the pilot's skill and the navigational instruments that supported it could read and conquer.[24] Fortunately, pilot, navigator, and plane were the best available, and the trip ended safely in the United States before Christmas—after 29,000 miles and five months of flying.

The Lindberghs arrived to a storm of controversy regarding congressional attempts to break up the "Airmail Trust." Senator Hugo Black of Alabama had gathered evidence that Walter F. Brown, postmaster general under the Hoover administration, had consolidated twenty-four of twenty-seven airmail contracts under three large holding companies, squeezing out many small businesses along the way. He informed President Franklin Roosevelt that the president could cancel contracts obtained by fraud or conspiracy. Roosevelt asked the chief of the Army Air Corps if the army could fly the mail should he do so. When General Benjamin Foulois said they could, the president immediately cancelled all airmail contracts, including those of Lindbergh's partners—Transcontinental and Western Airways (TWA). To add personal insult to commercial injury, Roosevelt's postmaster general, James A. Farley, said the airlines had overcharged the government nearly $47 million between July 1930 and January 1934, and much of the overpayment had gone to "The Lindbergh Line." Charles Lindbergh's part of that payment was his $20,000 annual salary and 25,000 shares of stock.[25] These personal references brought Charles into the fray.

On February 12, 1934, he released a telegram simultaneously to President Roosevelt and the newspapers. He asserted that the president's cancellation of airmail contracts constituted condemnation without just trial and lamented the endangerment to army pilots if they were forced to do a job they had not been trained for. Unfortunately for the president, Lindbergh's warning was prophetic, for in two months, twelve army pilots had died and forty-six more had experienced forced landings or injuries. In March, Lindbergh testified at Senate hearings for a bill designed to return airmail delivery to the commercial airlines. As Arthur Schlesinger, Jr., points out in *The Coming of the New Deal*, the passage of this bill was a major defeat for the administration, and the fight "uncovered in Charles Lindbergh a man who perhaps appealed to more American hearts than anyone save Franklin Roosevelt."[26]

If the victory over Roosevelt gave Lindbergh any satisfaction, he had little time to enjoy it. Developments on the kidnapping investigation began to pick up steam during the summer. With the help of a wood expert from the Department of Agriculture, police had traced the wood used in the kidnap ladder to its source. Simultaneously, gold notes from the ransom money began showing up at local banks. In one case, the owner of a service station had written the license number of a customer's car on the bill. Police found the car was registered to Richard Hauptmann, a German carpenter who lived in the Bronx. They found $13,000 more of Lindbergh's ransom money in his house and garage. One of the tools in his shop matched the square holes that had been punched in the original ransom note, and the chisel and wood left on the ground both led to him. Finally, Dr. Condon identified Hauptmann as the "John" he had seen at St. Raymond's Cemetery. In September 1934, Bruno Richard Hauptmann was arrested for the kidnap-murder of Charles Lindbergh, Jr.

Almost from the beginning, Hauptmann's arraignment and trial took on a circus atmosphere. More than 300 reporters attended the proceedings in Flemington, New Jersey, and three sacks of mail—ranging from sympathy to lurid threats—poured in to the Lindberghs' home every day. The prosecution's case, handled by state Attorney General David Wilentz, was a lengthy buildup of circumstantial evidence and personal testimony. Both Anne and Charles had to testify, but Charles was a central material witness because of his having heard "John" call "Hey, Doctor" in the cemetery. He clearly identified Hauptmann's voice as the one he had heard more than two years earlier.

Cross-examination by the defense attorney, Edward Reilly, was not particularly adept. He dwelled on two points: that someone inside the house could have committed the kidnapping and that few people would have known the Lindberghs intended to stay at Hopewell on that night, unless tipped off by an insider. Although these points argued for more than one person being involved in the crime, nothing could outweigh the mass of evidence from expert witnesses on Hauptmann's handwriting, the matching wood and tools, the money found at his home, and many more small details. On February 13, 1935, Hauptmann was convicted and sentenced to "death without mercy."

Lindbergh himself had gone disguised, day after day, to the trial. Sir Harold Nicolson, who was a guest at the Lindberghs' home during that time, found him almost possessed by the need to see and hear everything, perhaps to assure himself that Hauptmann was the guilty man. He describes how Charles went over the details of the case for Anne, who was distraught with uncertainty over the outcome. Charles said he had been concerned they would arrive at the end of the trial not knowing the truth, but that was not the case. Finally, he said, "There is no doubt at all that Hauptmann did the thing. . . . I am sure about this— quite sure."[27] The circumstantial conviction touched off some controversy, but both the New Jersey Court of Errors and Appeals and the State Supreme Court upheld the lower court's decision. Although Hauptmann won several stays of execution from Governor Harold Hoffman, he was finally put to death at the state prison in Trenton, still maintaining his innocence almost one year after his original sentencing.

While the final outcome was delayed during most of 1935, Charles busied himself with medical research. In June he published an announcement of spectacular success for his perfusion pump. He and Alexis Carrel had kept a cat's organs alive in the pump for months and, in fact, had observed the organs going through several cycles of life. A technical description of the pump appeared in the September issue of the *Journal of Experimental Science*, so the medical world could validate Lindbergh's results. Subsequent experiments showed that Charles had indeed achieved a major breakthrough for surgical medicine.

Unfortunately, all these public successes increased the pressure from reporters on the Lindberghs' private life. Their son, Jon, was living under tension, fear, and secrecy. One day, a black sedan had run his teacher's car off the road. It was full of newsreel and newspaper cameramen out for closeup pictures of Jon, even though Charles had a working agreement with the major newspapers not to publish his son's photograph. His picture appeared on the front page the next morning, and Charles had to take him from school and keep him at home under armed guard. This incident, as well as the unruly behavior of people following the kidnap trial, led him to observe later that "we Americans are a primitive people. . . . It shows in the newspapers, the morbid curiosity over crimes and murder trials. Americans seem to have little respect for law, or the rights of others."[28]

Because he respected the British regard for law and order and because he could not guarantee the security of his family against threats and extortionists, he announced to Deac Lyman of the *New York Times* that he was moving to England on December 22. The front-page story of his departure, which he asked Lyman to hold until his ship had been at sea twenty-four hours, won the reporter a Pulitzer Prize for journalism. It was a sensitive account of the public's harassment of the Lindbergh family and of the pressures that press curiosity had placed upon them. The *Herald Tribune* editorial that day hoped the Lindberghs would find a home "in a safer and more civilized land than ours has shown itself to be."[29]

LIFE IN EUROPE

For the next two years, the Lindberghs did find a more civilized place to live—Longbarn, Sir Harold Nicolson's house near Sevenoaks-Weald, in Kent. After an initial flurry of excitement among public and press, the British allowed them to settle down quietly, and Charles was able to take up his work in aviation once again.

By early 1936, European events made his interest in air power more vital. Germany had remilitarized the Rhineland, thus violating the Locarno Pact, and had begun to build the Luftwaffe into a modern air force. Although the Germans were producing obsolete planes for the time being, they had many new factories and the skeleton structure for massive production. In contrast, Lindbergh found the French aviation industry appalling. Official disinterest and frequent strikes had rendered their aircraft manufacturing plants almost useless. He decided to make a point of surveying the aircraft production of other European countries, because he believed the political balance would depend on air power.

By a happy confluence of circumstances, the U.S. Military Attaché in

Berlin, Major Truman Smith, was looking for a way to get Lindbergh to Germany as an observer. He sensed that the Luftwaffe was the vanguard of Germany's resurgence, but he was unable to obtain high-level air intelligence because he lacked experience and contacts with the top people in the German Air Ministry. He thought Lindbergh would be a catch for the Germans as they prepared for the 1936 Summer Olympics, especially since Hermann Goering, head of the Luftwaffe, liked celebrities. After clearing Lindbergh's visit with the air minister, General Erhard Milch, he wrote Charles to tell him that a tour of Germany that summer would be of high patriotic benefit from a purely American point of view. Lindbergh accepted, of course. He and Anne flew their new Miles "Mohawk" to Berlin in July.

Truman Smith had not mistaken Goering's eye for publicity. The Luftwaffe chieftain especially favored Lindbergh because of the aviator's prestige, mastery of air matters, and Swedish descent—his late wife was also Swedish. He invited the Lindberghs to attend opening day of the Olympics as his special guests, and he revealed many new aviation developments to Charles. Lindbergh noted that the Germans would not talk about rockets, so he surmised secret research was in progress. He also learned of the ME-109, a new fighter with impressive speed, armament, and flight ceiling, as well as the JU-87 "Stuka" dive bomber, which was to become the scourge of Poland, Czechoslovakia, and Dunkirk.

These weapons, coupled with a massive production capacity, convinced him that Germany had come of age in military aviation. In fact, he told Harold Nicolson later in the year that the Nazis had the most powerful air force in the world and that "if Great Britain supports the decadent French and the red Russians against Germany, there will be an end to European civilization."[30] To help guard against such a debacle, he recommended the British develop a deterrent bomber that could fly at 30,000 feet, be guided by the stars, and operate well at night. A weapon of this kind might discourage Germany from building a long-range air threat to complement its short-range dive bombers and fighters.

During the next two years, Lindbergh returned to Germany three times and also visited aircraft manufacturing plants and test facilities in Poland, Romania, Czechoslovakia, and the Soviet Union. In 1937, he learned of seven warplanes being tested at the Rechlin field in Pomerania—one of the most secret air fields in Germany—and discovered German plans for a two-engine fighter, the ME-110. In November, he helped Truman Smith prepare an estimate of Germany's air power for the U.S. General Staff. It showed Germany superior to France, nearly equal to Britain, and gaining on the United States. Although U.S. military authorities took the report seriously, the administration and the State Department did not.

By the end of 1938, Lindbergh had seen inferior air forces and poor production and maintenance throughout Europe and the Soviet Union. He wrote a letter to Joseph Kennedy, the U.S. ambassador to London, documenting the superiority of German air power. He saw the Luftwaffe as the strongest air force in the world, with a production potential of 20,000 planes a year, assuming they could obtain sufficient raw materials to maintain it. On the other hand, negligible or inefficient production was the rule in all other European nations, whose great cities would be threatened with extinction in the event of war.[31] Although Ambassador Kennedy cabled this information to the State Department, they never passed on his estimates to the War Department or the president.

In the meantime, the Lindberghs were increasingly uncomfortable away from the United States. They had moved to Iliec Island, off the French coast, soon after their third son, Land, was born in April, 1938. There, Charles had continued his association with Dr. Alexis Carrel, who lived on a neighboring island. They collaborated on *The Culture of Organs*, a book which summarized their experiments concerning perfusion of organs outside the body, as well as on several articles for the scientific community. The Lindberghs moved for a time to a Paris apartment, but the growing threat of war made living in Europe past the end of the year rather tenuous. Charles's outspoken remarks about German air superiority and his frequent appearances in Berlin also soured his reputation in France and England. Combined with a general feeling that they belonged back in their own country, where Charles might yet have some influence on military preparations, these events led them to return permanently to the United States in the spring of 1939.

RETURN TO CONTROVERSY

Charles had also written to General H. H. Arnold, chief of the Army Air Corps, recommending that General Arnold go to Germany to see their air force. He called for immediate development of high-speed aircraft in the U.S. to exceed the 400-mile-per-hour ceilings of most modern European pursuit craft. In April of 1939 he met with General Arnold at West Point to discuss the Luftwaffe and urge him to improve the American air force. Arnold placed him on extended active duty, put an Army P-36 at his disposal, and sent him to inspect aircraft manufacturing plants across the country. He attended the meeting of the National Advisory Committee for Aeronautics and helped them recommend to Congress a program for accelerated aircraft design and production, resulting in a $46 million appropriation to the War Department for more airplanes. His tours produced recommendations to the military aviation board for new and better military planes, as well as increased scientific research on weapons. Eventually, these were the armaments that won World War II for the United States.

Despite his sincere concern about building up the nation's defenses, Lindbergh was not pro-war. On the contrary, he hoped a defensive arsenal would dissuade other powers from attacking, thus preserving American democracy and Western culture from extinction. He believed the United States should enter or support the European war only if absolutely essential to the future welfare of the nation. Interestingly, most of the country joined him in these sentiments. More than 70 percent of the population were strongly pacifist in 1939, and nearly half were completely isolationist.[32] Thus when Fulton Lewis, Jr., asked Lindbergh to go on the radio to let the American people know how he felt, there was no reason to believe that his ideas would be anything but a confirmation of the prevailing national mood.

After Germany had invaded Poland, and England and France had declared war, Lindbergh decided to put his views as a private citizen ahead of his military duty by making a public speech against American involvement. As soon as he announced his intentions, President Roosevelt determined to head him off. The president wanted the 1937 Neutrality Act amended so he could give aid to France and England short of war. Lindbergh's popularity might help crystallize opinion against any change, thus blighting Roosevelt's plans. To avoid conflict, he first offered Charles a new position as Secretary of Air, but news of the offer did not filter through Secretary of War Woodring until just before Lindbergh's September 15 speech.[33] Charles declined, seeing it as an attempt to buy him off his anti-intervention position. Roosevelt also had the Internal Revenue Service investigate the aviator's tax returns, but Charles countered the move by opening them to the newspapers. He told reporters that it was a privilege to be an American, no matter what tax one paid, so he always instructed his accountants to drop borderline deductions, rather than to be vulnerable to challenge. Given Lindbergh's stubborn Swedish outlook, these two attempts could only have made him more determined to speak out.

Over the next two years, Charles became, according to Robert Sherwood, "Roosevelt's most formidable competitor on the radio."[34] He sounded out a few straightforward themes in his first speech, then gradually refined and clarified them in succeeding talks. He tied the shipping of armaments to eventual involvement—and loss—of American soldiers. He also believed that, once involved in this war, America would be tied to the future intrigue of European nations, even in peacetime. Instead, he felt America should rely temporarily on the oceans to separate the country from direct attack and begin building a defensive arsenal that would deter any adventuring in the years ahead. He warned the public against the "colored" views of the media and recommended they ask about owners and influencers, as well as writers and speakers, of radio stations, newspapers, and newsreel films.

To counter what he saw as the snowballing effect of administration reports and media hysteria, he mapped out four points of policy for the present conflict: embargoing export of offensive weapons and munitions, unrestricted selling of purely defensive armaments, prohibiting American shipping from the belligerent countries of Europe and their danger zones, and refusing credit to belligerent nations or their agents.[35] Finally, he published letters to Americans in *Reader's Digest* and *Collier's Magazine*, asking for careful analysis of any statement that urged the country toward involvement in the European conflict.

While Lindbergh spoke against involvement, first as a private citizen and then as a spokesman for the America First Committee, the Roosevelt administration was moving the country toward becoming the "arsenal of democracy." The president first used an 1892 statute that authorized the Secretary of War to lease army equipment when it was in the public good to do so. That allowed him to send $43 million worth of munitions and $20 million of overage destroyers to England. After being reelected in 1940, he was able to get the Lend-Lease Bill (H.R. 1776) passed through Congress, allowing him to lend or lease war materials to England and Russia beginning in 1941. By November 1941, he had gotten Congress to repeal more of the Neutrality Act, as well as to permit him to arm American merchant marine vessels and send them into war zones.

The administration also stepped up its attacks on Lindbergh during early 1941, partly because the Battle of Britain was illustrating both England's desperate position and her resolve to hang on against the Germans. Roosevelt's secretary of the interior, Harold L. Ickes, maintained an indexed file of all of Lindbergh's noninterventionist speeches, as well as a file of disparaging information about the aviator's visits to Berlin. In a series of public indictments, Secretary Ickes called Lindbergh "a peripatetic appeaser," the "No. 1 Nazi fellow traveler" in the United States, and "the first American to raise aloft the standard of pro-Naziism." Referring to a decoration Charles had received from Goering at a State dinner, he called him the "Knight of the German Eagle" for the work he had done to earn it.[36] In April, Roosevelt held a press conference to remark on Lindbergh as a spiritual leader of isolationism. He compared Charles to Vallandigham, a Copperhead, who had said the North could not win the Civil War and had made speeches against Lincoln. He also referred to the "summer soldiers and sunshine patriots" of the Revolutionary War—and he said he most certainly was talking about Lindbergh.[37] In other words, the administration began to refer to all those who opposed its policies as either traitors or Nazis.

Lindbergh reacted to these attacks in two ways. On April 28, 1941, he tendered his resignation as a colonel in the U.S. Air Corps Reserve, stating that Roosevelt's comments concerning his loyalty, character, and motives made it impossible to continue in the armed forces. To Secretary

Ickes's attacks, he wrote an open letter of rebuttal, addressed to President Roosevelt but previously released to the newspapers. In the letter he noted that he had had no contact with Nazi Germany since his last official visit, that he had received the decoration from Goering at a State function—arranged by the ambassador, and that Ickes owed him an apology for defamation of his character. Unfortunately, both actions played into the hands of the administration. His resignation was what Roosevelt wanted, without being forced to issue a public demand for it, and the letter delighted Secretary Ickes, because it showed that he had cracked Lindbergh's resolve not to respond to public criticism.

Charles stepped up his schedule of addresses, no matter the consequences. In an interview with Larry Kelly, of the New York *Journal-American*, he said he was speaking out despite the names he would be called and the damage to his personal life, because the future welfare of his country, family, friends, and fellow citizens was more important than the names one is called.[38] As Roosevelt won more and more concessions from Congress, however, his comments—as well as those of other speakers for America First—took on a shriller tone. Finally, on September 11, 1941, Lindbergh made an infamous speech at Des Moines naming the British, the Jews, and the Roosevelt administration as pushing the country inexorably toward war. He proclaimed sympathy for Jewish persecution but insisted that their pro-war policy and their large ownership and influence in motion pictures, press, radio, and government were a "great danger." Reaction was swift and inevitable. He was, indeed, called many names—Nazi, fool, and bigot among them— and his reputation was indelibly besmirched by them. Although he spoke again in October to an enthusiastic crowd of 20,000 people at Madison Square Garden, his effectiveness was diminished by vulnerability on "anti-Semitic" issues. Then too, the fate of the nation was rapidly becoming apparent. When Japan attacked Pearl Harbor on December 7, it was sealed, and Lindbergh's campaign against American intervention came to an end.

CONSULTING AND COMBAT—WORLD WAR II

On December 9, Lindbergh issued a statement to the press. He encouraged all Americans to meet the attack with a united front, despite prior differences over government policy. When American soldiers go to war, he said, they must do so with the best equipment that modern skill can design and that modern industry can build. To show his personal commitment to the defense of his country, he volunteered for readmission into the armed forces, but he was denied service—unless he were willing to recant his pre-war views.

Instead, he sought employment in the civilian aviation industry, hoping to help design and test new military airplanes. After successive turn-downs from United, Pan American, and Curtiss-Wright, he was finally invited by Henry Ford to work on the B-24 "Liberator" bomber in his plant at Willow Run, Michigan. The War Department approved Ford's offer, perhaps out of deference to the industrial giant's political clout. For the next year and a half, Charles worked as a $666-per-month technical consultant, making major improvements to the B-24's cockpit armor and gun turret operation. When he wasn't attending to the B-24, he exercised his practical interest in aerospace medicine to support the war effort. He conducted high-altitude experiments on himself to determine the effects of oxygen starvation on cognition and motor responses, and he tested the reliability and performance of the P-47's ignition system, also at high altitudes. Both activities led to improved in-flight equipment for pilots and crews.

Even without a combat record, these would have been significant accomplishments. But Lindbergh was eager to get into the action as a pilot, and in April of 1944 he got his chance. He managed to get to the South Pacific with the navy as a technical representative for United Aircraft Corporation—to test the F-4U "Corsair" fighter plane under combat conditions. Despite his nonofficial status, he joined the Marine Corsair squadron at Rabaul, helping to strafe ground targets and fly protective patrols. Later, he moved to New Guinea and the twin-engine P-38, joining Colonel Charles MacDonald and the 475th Fighter Group. MacDonald called Lindbergh "indefatigable. He flew more missions than was expected of a regular combat pilot . . . and was shot at by almost every anti-aircraft gun in western New Guinea."[39] Over Palau, he was attacked at close range. He poised to receive the enemy Zero's gunfire, but the Japanese pilot missed him completely. Finally, during one of his fifty combat missions, Lindbergh was credited with a kill of a Japanese Sonia-type fighter. With both pilots holding a head-on course, the two planes nearly collided, but the Sonia rolled over at the last second and smoked into the sea.

Although these combat experiences were important to Lindbergh, the aviator's technical advice played a much more impressive role in the war at large. He recommended fuel-saving techniques on the P-38 and a special bombing arrangement on the Corsair, thus increasing range and firepower for American forces. In fact, General George C. Kenney believed that his additions to the P-38's range allowed the United States to get to the Philippines much sooner, shortened the war by several months, and saved thousands of American lives.[40] Although his actions were not so well known as the famous transatlantic flight, Charles had become, once again, an American hero.

Opportunities to serve his country and aviation continued immediately after the war. In the spring of 1945 United Aircraft asked him to become a consultant on the Navy Technical Mission to Germany. His task was to study German developments in aircraft and missiles, with an eye to transferring technology and scientists to the United States. Because he was alarmed at Russian inroads to the German scientific community, his diaries from this period reflect several recommendations on acquiring key people for aerospace programs.

Lindbergh's general observations were tinged with sadness, however, because of the forced gaiety, tremendous destruction, and poor behavior by Allied troops toward hungry German women and children. He also remarked upon the filth and decay associated with the hordes of displaced people who roamed the country. Finally, he saw a concentration camp and factory near Nordhausen, where some 25,000 people had been thrown in incinerators after being worn out by labor. "Here was a place," he said, "where men and life and death had reached the lowest form of degradation."[41] Combined with the Americans' brutality toward Japanese soldiers in the South Pacific, this sight brought home to him the sickening results of war.

THE POST-WAR YEARS

When he returned from Germany, he decided it was time to establish a real home near Darien, Connecticut. His last child and second daughter, Reeve, was born in the fall, and his notoriety had dwindled, so a reasonably normal family life was now possible. He began commuting to New York, where he continued to work for Pan Am. Meantime, the children attended public school, and Anne wrote and oversaw their nine-bedroom, six-bath home on the waterfront.

Although Lindbergh was often gone on his travels for military and civilian aviation, he did spend some time with the children. His philosophy of child-rearing was, not surprisingly, much like his own father's dictum: freedom with responsibility. Thus, when Scott and Reeve intended to climb a particularly large tree in their yard, Charles told them to go ahead, but not before they planned it out to avoid as much risk as possible. His oldest son, Jon, benefitted equally from this advice. Jon handled a carving knife and fork when he was five, and he built his own projects with full-sized tools, much the way Charles did as a youngster. But in later years, when he got lost and came in far after dark from a day of lobstering, Lindbergh advised him not to overplay the odds. He also told Jon to take a life jacket and a compass when he went onto the water, thus always leaving himself more than one way out. Charles still believed some risk was necessary in life, but there was no use tempting fate by being foolhardy.

In addition to guiding his children's upbringing, Lindbergh was busy during the post-war years guiding the future of American airpower. At

General Carl (Tooey) Spatz's invitation, he became a civilian advisor to the military, commissioned to coordinate aerospace research and improve American defenses. For payment, he received a nominal salary of one dollar per year, an office in Washington, D.C., and a plane to get him around the country. He worked with the Strategic Air Command on crew selection procedures and development of strategic defense. For the Army's Ordnance Division, he participated in ballistic research, and as a member of the National Aeronautics and Space Administration (NASA) board, he encouraged concentrated work on missiles for space exploration—culminating his long-standing interest in Goddard's pioneering rocketry experiments. Early in 1949, he went to West Germany as an advisor to U.S. allied forces, to help overcome the Soviet blockade of Berlin. He recommended the most efficient operation of the Berlin Airlift and advised how to keep it flying past Soviet ground and air harassment. Because of these and many other accomplishments, Lindbergh received the Wright Brothers Memorial Trophy in 1949 for "significant public service of enduring evaluation to aviation and the United States."

Charles was pleased to accept the Wright Brothers Trophy, because he believed the country needed strong military defenses and technological progress to preserve society, at least until the moral fiber and vision of mankind caught up with its technology. Yet, in his acceptance speech, he stressed the urgency of balancing the "hothouse" achievements of science with the qualities of body, mind, and spirit. These two concerns had crystallized in his book, *Of Flight and Life*, published in 1948. One of its essays recounts Lindbergh's wartime high-altitude test in a P-47, during which a faulty gauge on his oxygen tanks nearly caused his death from anoxia. The experience, he said, taught him that "in worshipping science man gains power but loses the quality of life."[42] On the other hand, he thought, Americans represented the best of Western society, stemming from the culture of Greece and the teachings of Christ. Preserving that culture required its defense. Consequently, he believed that the country must be instructed by Western knowledge and protected by Western arms to preserve and progress.

Lindbergh's activities in the 1950s reflected this balanced view of life. He supported Douglas MacArthur in the Korean conflict, believing that the United States must stop communist aggression in the East as well as in the West. As a member of the Air Force Scientific Advisory Board, he increased emphasis on ballistic missile development. He spent much of his time at New Mexico and other proving grounds, and he helped Wernher von Braun and his colleagues translate German rocketry to U.S. programs. In 1954, he wrote an article for the *Saturday Evening Post* that argued the need for offensive strategic weapons to assure peace. As long as a dangerous enemy exists, he said, "our security will lie in our indestructible power to destroy." Although many disagreed with him, Lindbergh's remarks certainly revealed what would become the mainstream of strategic policy for the next three decades.

Charles viewed the machines of war as a necessary evil, but he saw manned spaceflight and progress in commercial flight as ways of avoiding conflict through international travel and cooperation. Thus, he remained active in NASA's space programs and in developing commercial aviation. His knowledge of space medicine, gained through demanding experiments on himself, particularly amazed early astronauts Michael Collins and Neil Armstrong. Because of his influence, a space medicine clinic was established at Brooks AFB, Texas, and most astronauts went through its rigorous testing in preparing for various space missions.

Lindbergh's work for Pan Am was equally impressive. He spurred production of Pratt and Whitney's giant J-75 jet engines and simultaneously interested Boeing and other airplane manufacturers in producing a new airframe to take advantage of their power. The result was an initial buy of more than 100 Boeing 707 aircraft in 1955. He also influenced major decisions on avionics and airfield support, as well as choices of additional locations for international service. Together, these changes helped usher in a new age of jet travel.

While the public Lindbergh carried on as a man of action, his private life was colored with contemplation, change, and some personal sorrow. In 1953, he published his Pulitzer Prize autobiography, *The Spirit of St. Louis*. Both its style and its content demonstrated significant growth in the author. Lindbergh's earlier account was spare—rooted in the bare actions and details of the transatlantic flight. This one was contemplative—using the exciting present-tense details to spark memories and imaginings of his relationship to nature and the world beyond. For the first time, the American public could fully understand what such a flight required of the pilot. Together with the equally literate film version of his story, which appeared in 1957, this best-selling autobiography brought the reality of his accomplishment to a new generation.

Other events in Lindbergh's life were not uniformly positive. On the plus side was his recommissioning in the United States Air Force. By direction of President Dwight Eisenhower, he was sworn in the reserve as a brigadier general, once more wearing the wings of an air force pilot. But later in 1954 he lost his mother, Evangeline Lodge Lindbergh, to heart and Parkinson's disease. Soon afterward, Anne Lindbergh's mother, Betty Morrow, died.

The death of her mother left Anne depressed and vaguely unhappy. Her children were less of an occupation, and Charles was seldom home from his travels, so she determined to live alone for a time at a southern beach cottage. Bird watching and searching for shells led to a book, *Gift from the Sea*, which was a balm for her spirit and a declaration of one woman's independent reunion with the natural world. Charles called it a beautiful little book, and it may well have rekindled his own deep feeling for nature. By 1967 he had decided that if he were entering adulthood at the time, he would choose a career in touch with nature more than science. In the Christmas issue of *Life* magazine, he said that he had "been forced to the conclusion that an overemphasis of science weakens character and upsets life's essential balance."[43] This conclusion grew ever more dominant in the years before his death in 1974.

THE LAST DECADE: TECHNOLOGY VS. CONSERVATION

During the 1960s, Lindbergh remained involved in technological progress, however. He revived his work on the perfusion of whole organs, updating his glass "pump" for cryobiological applications. Along with several navy investigators, he showed that organs could be frozen at extremely cold temperatures and then be "brought back to life" for use in operations.[44] He wrote forewords for two books that demonstrated his continuing interest in rocketry and the space program. His introduction to *This High Man*, by Milton Lomask, pays tribute to Robert Goddard, the great man of science and experimenter whose work in rocketry made space travel possible. And his foreword to *Vanguard: A History*, written in 1969, comments on his involvement in the American satellite program, which he thought might link the international community through better communications.

A similar impulse encouraged him to support the Apollo program and the supersonic transport. Each offered opportunities to bring world civilization closer together through mutual exploration and travel. When Lindbergh viewed the moon shot at Cape Kennedy in 1968, he saw it as the fulfillment of Robert Goddard's dream and marked it as a source of great contentment to him. Of course, Apollo also held the promise of heroic adventure on the last frontier, a prospect that induced Lindbergh briefly to consider active reentry into the field of astronautics. Science, especially when joined to risk and personal courage, still attracted him.

Despite the admirable advances of technology, though, the sixty-year-old Lindbergh moved resolutely beyond its realm to emphasize wilderness and the quality of natural life. While discussing the supersonic transport at a long technical conference in New York, he felt a sudden revulsion for the technological future. He left quickly, flew to Nairobi, and escaped within hours into the African bush—one of many jaunts into the wild during the last decade of his life. The irony of his trip—that without technology he could not have reached the wilderness so easily—was not lost on him. But, in a 1964 article for *Reader's Digest*, he said "that the construction of an airplane, for example, is simple when compared with the evolutionary achievement of a bird. . . . I realized that if I had to choose, I would rather have birds than airplanes."[45] In 1965 he joined the board of the World Wild Life Fund and the National Union for the Conservation of Nature, thus marking his official enlistment in conservation causes.

For the next several years, he was active in saving endangered species. He helped keep the blue and hump-backed whales from slaughter off the coast of Peru. The operation was controlled by an American in Minneapolis, a fellow Swede, who finally agreed with Lindbergh to stop harpooning the whales, so they could have time to replenish the herd. In 1968, he met a British wildlife activist named Tom Harrison at one of the World Wild Life Fund's Geneva meetings. Harrison, a natural rebel and feisty defender of right causes, had spent years in the jungles of Borneo studying wildlife. Like Alexis Carrel and Robert Goddard, he was committed to a life's work in his field of interest. Charles liked him immediately. He soon launched a fund-raising and political campaign to help Harrison save the tamarau and monkey-eating eagle of the Philippines.

Lindbergh's work in the Philippines brought him into contact with yet another organization—Panamin, or Private Association for National Minorities—which was devoted to saving the primitive Tasadays from civilization. The Tasadays were a Stone-Age tribe of Mindanao Island, who had no history, no religion, and no contact with the outside world until the 1960s. Most important in Lindbergh's mind was that they had no words for war, enemy, murder, or moral badness. Such a people, it seemed to him, needed to be preserved from exploitation.

As his last great adventure, at the age of seventy, he joined Manuel Elizalde, Jr., in an expedition to Tasaday country. He jumped from a helicopter into a treetop platform and climbed a steep cliff to the Tasaday caves, appearing little fazed by the arduous journey.[46] Once he had seen the friendly, innocent tribe, he was convinced they should continue living as they were. He obtained a proclamation from President Ferdinand Marcos that more than 46,000 acres of Tasaday country was to be a reserve—banned from outside exploitation, entry, sale, or lease. Having achieved his goal, Charles left the tribe in May 1972, never to return. His final tribute to them was a special exhibit, which he organized for the Smithsonian Institute later that year.

The next year, 1973, became a time of reaching into the past. Longer and more frequent visits to his beachside cottage in Maui led to more retrospective thinking and writing. Having published his wartime diaries in 1970, Charles continued to compile the details of his life, this time from the more philosophical perspective that arises from distance. They were to appear after his death as *An Autobiography of Values*, the title of the book indicating its reflective content. He also began writing letters to old friends he had not seen since before World War II, seeing it as a way of reconciling the rifts created by his anti-intervention views.

Finally, he attended dedications of Falaise, Harry Guggenheim's estate at Long Island, and of the Lindbergh State Park and Interpretive Center at Little Falls, Minnesota. Combined with the exhibitions of his exploratory flights at the Smithsonian Institution, where he visited often during the year, these monuments were the physical manifestations of his personal history.

None of these artifacts could hold back the march of moments, however, and time finally caught up with Lindbergh near the end of 1973. He came down with his first serious illness in years, suffering from a fever, rash, and loss of weight. Although he rallied somewhat in the spring, he spent the summer in Darien sweating and coughing. The cause, although he did not know it then, was lymphomatic infection and cancer. By August, he realized that he would not recover. He arranged to have himself flown to Maui, where he wished to be buried in a cemetery next to the Papala Hoomanu Congregational Church. He died at 7:15 A.M. on August 26, 1974, and was buried in plain work clothes three hours later. His simple eucalyptus casket was lined with a Hudson Bay blanket and placed in a deep tomb of lava rock, on a high promontory overlooking the sea. He lay facing the ocean and the sky, poised for his last long flight into the unknown.

NOTES

1. Several poems in Arthur Hooley, ed., *The Spirit of St. Louis: One Hundred Poems* (New York: George H. Doran, 1927) and numerous magazine and newspaper accounts of the flight.

2. Joseph Campbell, *The Hero With a Thousand Faces* (Princeton, New Jersey: Princeton University Press, 1949), chp. 1.

3. Lynn Haines and Dora B. Haines, *The Lindberghs* (New York: Vanguard Press, 1931), pp. 6-7. Other stories about August Lindbergh are from this source.

4. C. A. Lindbergh, *The Economic Pinch* (Philadelphia: Dorrance, 1923), pp. 162-163.

5. Kenneth S. Davis, *The Hero: Charles A. Lindbergh and the American Dream* (Garden City, New York: Doubleday, 1959), pp. 52-53.

6. Ibid., pp. 35-36.

7. Charles A. Lindbergh, *Boyhood on the Upper Mississippi* (St. Paul: Minnesota Historical Society, 1972), p. 2.

8. Walter S. Ross, *The Last Hero: Charles A. Lindbergh* (New York: Harper and Row, 1976), p. 3.

9. Lindbergh, *Boyhood*, pp. 11, 17.

10. Charles A. Lindbergh, *The Spirit of St. Louis* (New York: Charles Scribner's Sons, 1953), p. 255.

11. Charles A. Lindbergh, "And Then I Jumped," *Saturday Evening Post*, 200 (23 July 1927), pp. 6-7.

12. Lindbergh, *Spirit*, p. 308.

13. Ibid., p. 14.

14. Fitzhugh Green, "A Little of What the World Thought of Lindbergh," in Charles A. Lindbergh, *We: The Famous Flier's Own Story of His Life and Transatlantic Flight* (New York: G.P. Putnam's Sons, 1937), pp. 233-318.

15. Ross, *Last Hero*, p. 153.

16. Leonard Mosley, *Lindbergh: A Biography* (Garden City, New York: Doubleday, 1976), p. 126.

17. Anne M. Lindbergh, *Bring Me a Unicorn: Diaries and Letters of Anne Morrow Lindbergh, 1922-1928* (New York: Harcourt Brace Jovanovich, 1972), pp. 113-114.

18. Ross, *Last Hero*, p. 252.

19. See, for example, Charles A. Lindbergh, "Apparatus to Circulate Liquid Under Constant Pressure In a Closed System," *Science*, 73 (1931), p. 566; and Charles A. Lindbergh, "Method for Washing Corpuscles in Suspension," *Science*, 75 (1932), pp. 415-416. For a fuller account of the perfusion apparatus, see Charles A. Lindbergh, "An Apparatus for the Culture of Whole Organs," *The Journal of Experimental Medicine*, 62 (1 September 1935), pp. 409-431.

20. Anne Morrow Lindbergh, *North to the Orient* (New York: Harcourt Brace, 1935), pp. 28-35.

21. George Waller, *Kidnap* (New York: Dial Press, 1961), pp. 14-15. Succeeding information on the kidnapping is based almost exclusively on this definitive account.

22. Ibid., p. 223.

23. Ross, *Last Hero*, pp. 212-213.

24. Anne Morrow Lindbergh, *Listen! The Wind* (New York: Harcourt Brace, 1938), pp. 7-9.

25. Ross, *Last Hero*, pp. 255-259.

26. Arthur Schlesinger, Jr., *The Coming of the New Deal* (Boston: Houghton Mifflin, 1958), p. 355.

27. Sir Harold Nicolson, *Diaries and Letters: 1930-1939* (New York: Atheneum, 1966), p. 197.

28. As quoted in Roger Butterfield, "Lindbergh: A Stubborn Young Man of Strange Ideas Becomes a Leader of Wartime Opposition," *Life*, (11 August 1941), p. 65.

29. Waller, *Kidnap*, p. 600.

30. Nicolson, *Diaries and Letters*, p. 262.

31. Truman Smith, Col., USA (ret.), "Air Intelligence Activities, Office of the Military Attaché, American Embassy, Berlin, Germany, August 1935-April 1939, with special reference to the Services of Colonel Charles A. Lindbergh, Air Corps Reserve" (Unpublished Manuscript: Yale University Library, 1954-1956), pp. 140-142.

32. Ross, *Last Hero*, p. 295—quoting the Gallup Poll of September 1939.

33. Mosley, *Lindbergh*, pp. 257-259.

34. Robert E. Sherwood, *Roosevelt and Hopkins* (New York: Harper and Brothers, 1948), p. 153.

35. Charles A. Lindbergh, *The Radio Addresses of Colonel Charles A. Lindbergh* (Lake Geneva, Wisconsin: *Scribner's Commentator*, 1940), pp. 2-8.

36. As quoted in Wayne S. Cole, *Charles A. Lindbergh and the Battle Against Intervention in World War II* (New York: Harcourt Brace Jovanovich, 1974), pp. 130-133.

37. Ross, *Last Hero*, p. 311.

38. As reported in ibid., p. 319.

39. Colonel Charles MacDonald, "Lindbergh in Battle," *Collier's*, 117 (16 February 1946), p. 12.

40. General George C. Kenney, Interview with the Boston *Sunday Advertiser*, 1 September 1957, as quoted in Ross, *Last Hero*, p. 332.

41. Charles A. Lindbergh, *The Wartime Journals of Charles A. Lindbergh* (New York: Harcourt Brace Jovanovich, 1970), pp. 997-998.

42. Charles A. Lindbergh, *Of Flight and Life* (New York: Charles Scribner''s Sons, 1948), p. 10.

43. Charles A. Lindbergh, "Wisdom of Wildness," *Life*, 63 (22 December 1967), pp. 8-10.

44. Charles A. Lindbergh, With V. P. Perry et al., "An Apparatus for the Pulsating Perfusion of Whole Organs," *Cryobiology*, 3 (1966), pp. 252-260.

45. Charles A. Lindbergh, "Is Civilization Progress?" *Reader's Digest*, 25 (July 1964), pp. 67-74.

46. Mosley, *Lindbergh*, p. 385.

2

LINDBERGH, AVIATION, AND AMERICAN SOCIETY

Charles Lindbergh is in many ways a prototype of twentieth-century America. His origin in what had recently been the Minnesota frontier and his enduring love of wilderness and farm represent a rural impulse—an impulse that still persists in national parks, mountain retreats, and, perhaps diluted, in campgrounds and suburbia. At the same time, his continuing interest in science and mechanics suggests the technological progress of America, whose complex institutions make modern society possible.

As a number of commentators on American culture have noted, this schizophrenic attitude is typical of America throughout its development, but it became particularly intense at the beginning of this century.[1] Henry Adams crystallized the tension between traditional values and progress in *The Education of Henry Adams*. He suggested that the unifying moral force of medieval Christianity had given way to a multiplistic force characterized by the dynamo, or flywheel-driven generator, displayed at the Chicago Exposition of 1893. This electro-mechanical device, quietly and perpetually humming, seemed to generate a force totally independent of "human" qualities. Adams predicted that modern society would worship at the dynamo rather than the statue of the Virgin and would thus establish the supremacy of mechanistic principles over the intuitive unity of religion and moral values.[2] Industrialization and urbanization in America appear to have validated this prediction. On one hand, Americans celebrate the individualism and self-sufficiency represented by frontiersmen or homesteaders. On the other, we admire the technical ingenuity, mechanization, and corporate power which subsume individual achievement into national progress.

Few activities combine these impulses more neatly than flight. Even before Lindbergh's transatlantic junket, the airplane had captured the imagination of many Americans. The barnstorming era produced its share of regional "heroes" and offered those who could pay for a ride the chance to slip the bonds of earth. Songs, poems, and popular novels pictured the airplane as a romantic vehicle into adventure and, after World War I began, into patriotic combat. But these activities were individual sport. Even combat was pictured as a series of "boxing matches" between great flyers. Nothing in them welded the wondrous invention to a sense of national purpose.

THE HEROIC EXPLORER AND ENTREPRENEUR

Lindbergh's early career in flight provided a focus that had been lacking before he piloted the *Spirit of St. Louis* from New York to Paris. Lindbergh became a type representing the energy and high purpose of the United States, at a time when that purpose seemed to be mired in sensationalism and political corruption. As John W. Ward suggests in "The Meaning of Lindbergh's Flight," this one achievement became "a public act of regeneration in which the nation momentarily rededicated itself to something the loss of which was keenly felt."[3] Above all, this something was the ideal of a pioneering, self-sufficient individualism, which permeates American history. In commenting on Lindbergh's transatlantic flight, the *Nation* observed that "there was something lyric as well as heroic about the apparition of this young Lochinvar who suddenly came out of the West and who flew all unarmed and all alone. . . . What we have in the case of Lindbergh is an actual, an heroic and an exhaustively exposed experience which exists by suggestion in the form of poetry."[4]

Other writers emphasized Lindbergh's origin in rural solitude to suggest that such a spirit could grow only in isolation from the formal institutions of modern society. Joseph K. Hart in *Survey* magazine stressed the flyer's "audaciously natural and simple personality" and his "pioneering urge," which contrasted to the 99 percent of us who "must be content to be shaped and moulded by the routine ways and forms of the world to the routine tasks of life."[5] In the tremendous public acclaim for Lindbergh that welled up from the nation's great cities, Hart saw a "homesickness of the human soul, immured in city canyons and routine tasks, for the freer world of youth, for the open spaces of the pioneer, for the joy of battling with nature and clean storms once more on the frontiers of the earth." In one view, then, Lindbergh was a lineal descendant of great American pioneers like Daniel Boone or Davy Crockett, because he blazed a path into the new frontier of the air.

Of course Lindbergh's actual achievements were bound less to the heroic past than to the progressive future. As in all pioneering efforts, his flights were part of the technology that preceded them and precursors of an increasingly complex civilization that followed. In fact, Lindbergh was more akin to Captain John Smith or Benjamin Franklin than to the lone woodsmen of the West. Like Smith, he was aware of the possibilities for enterprise on this new frontier. Smith's writings reflect a keen concern for development of timber, fishing, and fertilizer industries in the Virginia and New England wilderness. His explorations, mapping, and Indian fighting were part personal adventure and part social duty if civilization was to be expanded into America.[6] Similarly, Lindbergh saw aviation was a pleasure and a business, first to establish or expand commercial mail or cargo delivery and then to develop passenger service throughout the world. He did not wander aimlessly through the skies after 1927. He prepared carefully and planned the most direct routes to distant places.

Benjamin Franklin's life may well have influenced Charles directly. Like Franklin, Lindbergh constructed a list of "rules" to live by. But neither man considered honesty and business success to be mutually exclusive. Just as Franklin tinkered incessantly with mechanical devices to improve the quality of human life, so Lindbergh either invented or spurred the invention of life-saving implements in aircraft, electronics, navigational aids, and medicine. Franklin's mapping of the streets of Philadelphia in anticipation of its growth into a great city is similar to Lindbergh's diligent mapping and recording of geographical, atmospheric, and facilities support details, which led to a modern transportation system. Like Smith and Franklin, he also spent the last decades of his life in service to his nation and the world at large. Without pushing these parallels too far, one can say that all three were public men whose visions were tied to the progress of society.

The technological advances implicit in America's social progress were also intrinsic to Lindbergh's career in aviation. Lindbergh himself drew attention to the wonderful Wright motor that carried him across the Atlantic. He always said "we" when speaking of this flight to emphasize the machine and his "silent partners" in American industry. Indeed, the *New York Times* referred to the aviator as a symbol of the mechanical genius which was in the very atmosphere of America and described him as "the Icarus of the twentieth century; not himself an inventor of his own wings, but a son of that omnipotent Daedalus whose ingenuity has created the modern world."[7] Calvin Coolidge also stressed American industry in his speech accompanying the award of the Distinguished Flying Cross to Lindbergh. He noted that more than 100 separate companies had provided materials, parts, or service in the construction of the *Spirit of St. Louis*.[8] Numerous company and trade magazines hailed the flight as a culmination of aeronautical research and industrial techniques, which had been developed by engineers through twenty years of patient and extended effort. In this view Lindbergh's spontaneous heroism, though still significant, was subordinate to the power, organization, and planning necessary to industrial society.

These two contradictory analyses of Lindbergh's flight are pertinent to the aviator's own development. His career was a balance between individual effort and corporate involvement. Sheer love of flying and an adventurous spirit certainly motivated him to take several long tours, but each of these flights served commercial aviation as well. The first of these undertakings, for example, was his forty-eight-state, eighty-two-city tour of America in the fall of 1927, planned along with Harry Guggenheim and the Department of Commerce to promote aeronautics. The trip gave a tremendous boost to air mail and commercial aviation. By the end of 1930 the United States had witnessed a 70 percent growth in landing fields and airports, some 600 more lighted airstrips, and an 80 percent increase in pounds of mail carried. Many of the smaller cities that decided to build community airports credited their decisions to Lindbergh's activities and his personal appeals to expand modern facilities.[9] He emphasized mapping, planning, and punctual arrival at his destinations to show that airplane travel was safe and routine. Only by playing down the romantic thrill of risking life and limb could he convince the public to invest money and faith in aeronautics. This investment, in turn, transformed aviation from recreation or entertainment to large-scale business.

CONTRIBUTIONS TO COMMERCIAL AVIATION

In the continental United States, airmail and passenger service took a large leap forward with the development of Transcontinental Air Transport in 1928. Lindbergh and his St. Louis partners—Harold Bixby, Harry Knight, and Bill Robertson—conceived of a New York to Los Angeles service at a time when cost analysis showed that a profit was not possible while carrying passengers in airplanes. To attract passengers, mail, and freight in profitable quantities, airplanes would have to be faster, safer, and more reliable than the best being produced. Also, it was nearly impossible to fly safely over mountain ranges and at night with present equipment. Finally, to launch such a venture would require millions of dollars for capital investment, both to build facilities and to sustain their operation through the less profitable early years. Somehow, they would have to solve these problems before a dream could become reality.

Fortunately, two solutions made the line operational by July 1929. The Ford company began to produce trimotor aircraft which could handle Pratt and Whitney's 400-horsepower Wasp engines—sufficiently large and powerful to carry twelve passengers at a cruising speed of 105 miles per hour. Lindbergh chose these planes over wood-winged Fokkers, because they would be easier to maintain. He also rejected Boeing and

Curtiss transports because they were biplanes, which were overly subject to icing in flight and to wallowing in turbulent air, as well as to excessive maintenance under daily operation. As chairman of the airline's technical committee, Lindbergh made or influenced every important decision concerning aircraft selection, routing, and ground support.

Problems with night operations and financing found their solution in a creative union between trains and airplanes. The St. Louis businessmen spoke to Clement Keys, chief executive of the Curtiss Airplane Company, about financing their scheme. Keys was an important figure in the aviation financial world, with contacts in other areas of transportation, such as the railroads. Through Keys, the group was able to get financial backing from the Pennsylvania Railroad and to use trains in their first transcontinental passenger network. The final plan called for night railway service from New York to Columbus, Ohio, and from Waynoka, Oklahoma, to Clovis, New Mexico. This night service alternated with two daylight plane flights, on which stops were made at Indianapolis, St. Louis, Kansas City, Wichita, Albuquerque, Winslow (Arizona), and Kingman. Although these arrangements were primitive by today's standards, the "Lindbergh Line" saved transcontinental passengers twenty-four hours over the all-rail trip, which had been a seventy-two-hour venture. With government subsidies for mail delivery and increasing passenger use, TAT eventually grew and became Transworld Airlines (TWA), one of this country's largest air carriers.

Among Lindbergh's significant influences on TWA was his contribution to the design of one of aviation's legendary planes: the Douglas DC-series transport. In 1932, TWA had asked Douglas to produce a new passenger plane that would replace the outmoded trimotors then in service. Lindbergh argued that the design should allow the twin-engine plane to take off on a single engine, fully loaded, from any station along TWA's routes. Douglas stretched his company's engineering skills to achieve Lindbergh's goal with the DC-1. Encouraging performance led to the larger-capacity DC-2 and then to the exceptionally successful DC-3, which is still being flown in many countries today. Lindbergh's insistence on advanced designs to assure maximum safety and economy was a major impetus to early passenger service in the United States.[10]

Lindbergh's association with international aviation helped foster an even more dramatic growth in size and complexity. Juan T. Trippe, president of Pan Am, points out that Lindbergh understood from the start the technical, economic, and political requirements of commercial flying.[11] He describes Lindbergh's contributions as a product of verve and vision. The first air mail flights to South America in 1929 were in relatively small Sikorsky "flying boats," with engines that had only recently become reliable enough to consider regular long-distance service. Moreover, Lindbergh was warned that it would be foolhardy to fly in the Caribbean, because the weather was bad and unpredictable, with rain squalls too frequent and heavy to fly through. Combined with long routes over water, rugged forests, and rocky highlands, these dangers made Lindbergh's efforts extremely hazardous.

Similar difficulties plagued the Lindberghs' two long exploratory flights in the 1930s. In 1931, with Anne acting as radio operator and navigator, the Lindberghs reached the Orient via the great circle route over the Arctic and down to Japan and China. This polar route, essentially similar to the one followed by airliners today, was fraught with ice fogs, difficult winds, and spotty communications. Blind flying and forced landings were part of the "excitement."

In 1933, the Lindberghs again flew a pioneering survey flight to Greenland, Europe, Russia, Africa, and South America to map out commercial air routes across the North and South Atlantic. Lindbergh developed a special "sky hook" to gather air samples, completed air surveys for landing fields, and drew up plans for radio and meteorological stations to provide ground support for international travel. Anne's accounts of these two trips, in *North to the Orient* (1935) and *Listen! The Wind* (1938), show that they were often at risk—creeping in and out of mountain valleys to find their way to a safe harbor among the jagged rocks and dashing waves, flying into blinding ice storms and fog, and narrowly escaping serious accidents. But, as was usual for Lindbergh, months of careful planning, prepositioning of fuel and supplies, a touch of luck, and no little flying skill brought them through safely.

More important than Lindbergh's personal risk-taking, however, were his technical knowledge and his understanding of the direction commercial air transport should take. According to Trippe, he was among the first to envisage fares sufficiently low to allow the average person to travel by air. To ensure that people would do so, he insisted Pan Am not start a route unless they were able to maintain it under all conditions. Economic feasibility, reliability, and safety were equally necessary to their operations, and Lindbergh stressed each in his plans. Although he recognized land planes would eventually replace flying boats on transoceanic flights, he recommended the latter for early operations. Since experience alone could determine the best air routes and support locations, he wanted to keep fixed costs to a minimum until the routes were fully established. A flying boat operation gave commercial carriers flexibility with least cost. Lindbergh pointed out that meteorological knowledge, as well as improvements in engine design, radio, flight instruments, and operating techniques, could easily be transferred to land planes when the time was right. Meantime, Pan Am could begin and expand routes almost overnight as demand required.

Largely because of Lindbergh's technical requirements, which expanded the boundaries of engineering design, commercial aviation underwent remarkable growth between 1929 and 1939. In this flying boat era alone, aircraft power and size increased eight fold in support of Pan Am's overseas routes. Horsepower grew from 840 to 6200, maximum weight from 10,480 to 84,480 pounds, and range from 300 to 2400 miles. Increases in range and payload made transpacific and transatlantic service possible, thus opening up every continent to the exchange of goods and peoples.

During the 1930s Lindbergh was also active in national aeronautical research. He became a member of the National Advisory Committee for Aeronautics (NACA), forerunner to the National Aeronautics and Space Administration (NASA). He conferred frequently with aviation experts on various problems and was even asked if he would accept the committee chairmanship in 1939. He declined because he felt his greatest interests lay in other fields and because he did not wish to devote all his attention to aviation. As an active member of the committee, however, he insisted on a comprehensive national policy for aeronautical research and development, one aimed at keeping American aircraft competitive with foreign counterparts. He was also a driving force behind the Ames Aeronautical Laboratory. He chaired the committee on the laboratory proposal and argued for its usefulness despite aircraft industry opposition. Now incorporated under NASA as the Ames Research Center, this facility has greatly influenced American aerospace development, especially in reentry technology vital to exploring space.[12] Together with his support of Robert Goddard's pioneering efforts in rocket propulsion, discussed earlier, these activities illustrate how Lindbergh's influence permeated early aeronautical progress in America.

As passenger service moved into the jet age, Lindbergh continued to lead the advancement of commercial aviation. Before World War II he had been one of the first advocates of turbojet development, largely as a safety booster if conventional designs should fail. Soon after the war, he became convinced that the jet would eventually make the piston engine obsolete for long-range flights. By 1950 he was working with Boeing, Douglas, Pratt and Whitney, and others on designs for a transoceanic jet to supplant piston-engine planes operating on around-the-world routes. He rejected Boeing's plan to offer Pan Am a civilian version of the KC-135 jet tanker. The plane was too small, with too few seats and insufficient range to support a first-class transoceanic schedule. Eventually, he helped Pan Am obtain 116 large jet engines (Pratt and Whitney J-75s), which were to be used in a new aircraft designed to their specifications. Both Douglas and Boeing agreed to try. In 1955 Pan Am signed orders for forty-five Boeing 707s, and three years later the first jet service by any U.S. airline began, appropriately enough, with a New York to Paris flight.

Although these efforts are not so dramatic as Lindbergh's exploratory flights, they do show his adaptability and dedication to aeronautical advancement in America. The last two decades of his life mark an interminable number of corporate meetings, technical studies, and flights to various corners of the world in support of Pan Am's international growth. The pure joy and adventure of his earlier missions gave way to the monotony of long flights in "flying buses," as Lindbergh called them. But even though traveling as a passenger on Pan Am's routes did not appeal to him personally, he was convinced that tourism could help bring down international barriers. He wanted to break up the prejudices between nations by linking them through aviation. For this reason, he pushed for development of the Boeing 747 Jumbojet and, as a member of Pan Am's Board of Directors, was instrumental in their approving its purchase in 1966. By the late 1970s, the 747 was carrying approximately 90 percent of America's international traffic—carrying more passengers at a lower cost than ever before. If Lindbergh's ideal of international cooperation remains elusive, one cannot fault his vision, his efforts, or his successes in civilian aviation.

CONTRIBUTIONS TO MILITARY AVIATION

Less well known, except to those who worked with Lindbergh, are his numerous contributions to military aviation in the United States. His enlistment in the Army Air Corps training program began a lifelong association with the Department of Defense. He was Captain Lindbergh, of the Missouri National Guard, when he flew alone across the Atlantic. After being promoted immediately to colonel, he retained his commission until April 1941, when disagreement with Roosevelt's policies forced him to resign. But despite his resignation, he never really divorced himself from the military establishment. His significant contributions to aircraft and missile development continued until the last years of his life.

Lindbergh's interest in military aviation grew from the ominous necessities of World War II. Beginning in 1936 he personally flew nearly every military plane available to such countries as Britain, France, Russia, Czechoslovakia, Poland, Germany, and, of course, the United States. He provided the government valuable intelligence on German developments, including their advanced ME-109 single-wing fighter, and became the leading technical expert on European air power. As a special assistant to General H. H. Arnold in 1939, he toured defense plants and laboratories in the U.S. to establish aircraft production policies, advise on technical designs, and promote better facilities. Arnold found this aid invaluable to America's eventual preparation for the war.

Once war was declared, Lindbergh immediately volunteered his services. Barred from military duty by Roosevelt's instructions to the War Department, he worked as a civilian consultant for Henry Ford's B-24

Liberator bomber project at Willow Run, Michigan. He discovered that its armor plate was insufficient to protect its crews and that many of the aircraft were improperly assembled. He meticulously gathered data and directed production changes to avoid future problems of the same kind. Equal care was evident on other military projects Lindbergh undertook. He risked his life to run high-altitude ignition tests of the P-47, diligently worked out solutions for cylinder head problems in a radial aircraft engine designed for the Army Air Corps by Pratt and Whitney, and studied turbojet design with engineers of the Vought Company, hoping to produce turbo boosters for American military and civilian aircraft.[13] In all these endeavors he was willing to endure exhausting schedules, even under threat of death, because he recognized the implications of technological research for America's war readiness.

Besides these and other accomplishments in the early years of the war, Lindbergh served as a combat pilot in F4U Corsairs and P-38 Lightnings during the last half of 1944. Although he was to be solely a civilian observer, he managed to fly fifty combat missions before having to return to the United States. His techniques for improved fuel economy, which he had practiced on the New York to Paris flight, became a key to extended combat radius and greater Allied effectiveness against the Japanese.

As a consultant to the Naval Technical Mission just after the war, Lindbergh studied Nazi developments in aircraft and missiles. He recommended that the United States bring many of Germany's experts to this country to work in American programs for aerospace research, because his experiences in combat had taught him that "without a highly developed science modern man lacks the power to survive."[14] Unfortunately, despite his awareness that militarism had run amuck in Germany, he recognized that science must apply itself to deterrent force as well as to material progress. In 1945 he worked with Army Ordnance at the University of Chicago on a secret project called CHORE, which produced an influential study on developing new air-to-air weapon systems. He drew on his technical knowledge of flight and navigation to map efficient methods of operation for the Berlin Airlift, participated with the Air Force Scientific Advisory Board in studies of nuclear weapons and ballistic missiles, and served as a member of the advisory board panel on ballistic missile defense. Although he occasionally got into the action, such as in his several airplane rides to East Berlin, most of these associations called for endless planning projects, carried out in stuffy boardrooms, as well as a commitment to producing massive unmanned weapons to preserve freedom.[15]

With the responsibilities of a nuclear age resting on Western society, Lindbergh became increasingly concerned about the quality of men entrusted with military power. Thus, he began to consult with the air force on ways to increase the combat efficiency of the Strategic Air Command (SAC). He inspected and helped reorganize SAC's bases, took familiarization flights in B-52 bombers, and flew on twenty-hour training missions with the 509th Atomic Bomb Group out of Walker Air Force Base, New Mexico. He insisted that SAC should receive exceptional priorities in selecting officers or crews and that command people be kept on station for longer periods to improve their knowledge of operations. He also believed they should have training in emergency procedures at least monthly and that every SAC pilot should fly basic trainers periodically to maintain proficiency.[16] As a member of the committee to select a site for the United States Air Force Academy, he recommended rigorous selection criteria for cadets and a balanced curriculum to develop their leadership abilities. All these concerns were a counterpoise to the mathematical objectivity of ordnance and ballistic studies, in which human beings had become mere "bodies" on analog computer readouts.

SPACE AND BEYOND

Eventually, Lindbergh became enthralled with manned space flight. It appeared to offer another frontier for a courageous, visionary mankind, with the possibility of connecting people not only between countries but throughout the universe. When the Apollo 8 spacecraft lifted off toward its flight around the moon in 1968, Lindbergh saw it as vindication of Robert Goddard's great pioneering research and long travail. At that moment, he felt an "almost overwhelming desire to reenter the field of astronautics." But he resisted the urge because decades spent with "science and its vehicles" had directed his "mind and senses to an area beyond their reach."[17] He hoped space exploration would join the world's people in common enterprise. But, in truth, he had begun a different sort of "flight" beyond the bounds of scientific research.

Perhaps a fitting way to finish an assessment of Lindbergh's contributions in aviation is to note his final understanding of its limitations. By 1969, he had decided that the great adventures of the future would lie in "the application of our scientific knowledge not to life's mechanical vehicles but to the essence of life itself."[18] So he turned his attention from technological progress to preserving the wild, from embracing advances in aeronautics to a guarded recognition of their necessity in a modern world. In 1973, he addressed people attending the dedication of the Lindbergh Interpretive Center in Little Falls, Minnesota. The conclusion to his speech reaffirmed his belief in nature as our primary value:

On this riverbank one can look upward in late evening and watch a satellite penetrate through stars, thereby spanning human progress from the primitive hunter with his canoe to the latest advance of our civilization. . . . I believe our civilization's latest advance is symbolized by the park rather than by satellite and space travel. In establishing parks and nature reserves, man reaches beyond the material values of science and technology. He recognizes the essential value of life itself, of life's natural inheritance irreplaceably evolved through earthly epochs, of the miraculous spiritual awareness that only nature in balance can maintain.[19]

This balance of technical expertise and spiritual vision is Charles Lindbergh's legacy to America.

NOTES

1. See Leo Marx, *The Machine in the Garden: Technology and the Pastoral Idea in America* (New York, 1964), for a full discussion of this phenomenon.

2. Henry Adams, *The Education of Henry Adams: An Autobiography* (Dunwoody, Georgia: Norman S. Berg, 1975), pp. 379-390 and 474-488.

3. John W. Ward, "The Meaning of Lindbergh's Flight," *American Quarterly*, 10 (1958), p. 7.

4. As quoted in ibid., p. 8.

5. Joseph K. Hart, "O Pioneer!" *Survey*, 58 (1 July 1927), pp. 384-385.

6. See Edward Arber and A. G. Bradley, eds., *Travels and Works of Captain John Smith* (Edinburgh: John Grant, 1910) for his writings on the Virginia and New England colonies of the early seventeenth century.

7. "Lindbergh Symbolizes the Genius of America," *New York Times*, as quoted in Ward, "Meaning," p. 13.

8. Calvin Coolidge, *Address Bestowing on Charles A. Lindbergh the Distinguished Flying Cross* (Washington, D.C.: U.S. Government Printing Office, 1927), p. 2.

9. Walter Ross, *The Last Hero* (New York: Harper and Row, 1976), pp. 159-160. See also Richard P. Hallion, *Legacy of Flight: The Guggenheim Contribution to American Aviation* (Seattle: University of Washington Press, 1977), pp. 152, 154-158, 159.

10. Richard P. Hallion, "Charles A. Lindbergh and Aviation Technology," in *Charles A. Lindbergh: An American Life*, ed. Tom Crouch (Washington, D.C.: National Air and Space Museum, 1977), p. 44.

11. Juan T. Trippe, *Charles A. Lindbergh and World Travel* (New York: Wings Club "Sight" Lecture Series, 1977), p. 10. The next three paragraphs depend upon this source, pp. 10-19.

12. Hallion, "Aviation Technology," pp. 44-45.

13. Charles A. Lindbergh, *The Wartime Journals of Charles A. Lindbergh* (New York: Harcourt Brace Jovanovich, 1970), pp. 609-773, passim.

14. Charles A. Lindbergh, *Of Flight and Life* (New York: Charles Scribner's Sons, 1948), p. 14.

15. Leonard Mosley, *Lindbergh: A Biography* (Garden City, New York: Doubleday, 1976), pp. 345-346.

16. Judith A. Schiff, "Values of Flight and Life: The Postwar Activities," in Crouch, *An American Life*, p. 73.

17. Charles A. Lindbergh, "A Letter from Lindbergh," *Life*, 67 (4 July 1969), p. 60A.

18. Ibid., p. 61.

19. Charles A. Lindbergh, "Some Remarks at the Dedication of Lindbergh State Park Interpretive Center," *Minnesota History*, 43 (Fall 1973), p. 276.

3

LINDBERGH IN
POPULAR CULTURE

The public reaction to Charles Lindbergh has been phenomenal, even by modern standards of inflated emotions and media coverage. This phenomenon grew not only from his accomplishment of flying the Atlantic alone but also from his character. Each of his natural gestures sent a wave of newspaper coverage and public approbation around the world. A telephone call to his mother from Paris to Detroit, his visit to the lost Nungesser's mother, his praise of Nungesser and Coli's attempt on the Atlantic as far greater than his own—all showed he was unspoiled by success. Modesty, honesty, refusal to be tempted by money or fame, and a combination of naivete and sincere appreciation for the accolades of the people won over millions in every country he visited.

The official receptions and speeches—which thousands attended in France, England, Belgium, and the United States—caught some of Lindbergh's meaning for contemporary society. At a luncheon given by the Air Council in London, Sir Samuel Hoare observed that the peoples of many nations applauded Lindbergh's achievement because it was a "fine example of nerve and endurance, of skill, courage, enterprise, and adventure."[1] These qualities were especially uplifting to people in the United States, because they thought of themselves as partners in the enterprise. When Mayor Jimmy Walker welcomed Lindbergh to New York, for example, he helped define the public's part in the aviator's accomplishment. Walker stressed that every American heart and every soul throughout the world was riding with Lindbergh on his transatlantic journey, urging him and cheering him on to the great feat that was his.[2]

This idea of Lindbergh's flight as both private and public event was bolstered by President Calvin Coolidge's speech accompanying the award of the Distinguished Flying Cross. The president referred to him as a "genuine exemplar of fine and noble virtues," who had returned unspoiled to the cheers of his countrymen, but he also emphasized the contributions of more than 100 American companies and the technical expertise of engineers, builders, and mechanics in support of the flight.[3] His exploit thus combined the best aspects of moral character, frontier adventure, and industrial science—the accepted elements of American greatness.

By the time Lindbergh arrived home on the *U.S.S. Memphis*, he had become a national type and an international hero. Bells, factory whistles, automobile horns, fire sirens, and the guns of shore batteries joined in saluting his return, while many of the crowd wept with joy to see him. More than a million people massed in Washington, D.C., to view him, and hundreds of thousands staged demonstrations in his honor as he flew above them on the way to New York. But the most overwhelming reception was in New York City, where some 300,000 people gathered at the Battery in the harbor and more than 4 million crowded the streets and Central Park for his tickertape parade.[4] At a dinner later that week, a speaker emphasized what such demonstrations meant to the city, the press, and the United States. Lindbergh had displaced all that was petty, sordid, or vulgar and had brought America to contemplate the noblest and the best—when "science and character join hands to lift up humanity with a vision of its own dignity."[5] Perhaps that is why, at the end of one week in his home country, Lindbergh had inspired more than 2 million letters and several hundred thousand telegrams touting his deeds and character.

NEWSPRINT JOURNALISM

If Charles represented these elements, certainly the press helped shape them into an epic view that captured the public imagination. During the first month following his flight, American newspapers expended on him more than 25,000 tons of newsprint above their normal consumption. Coverage of his receptions in Europe, which drew half a million people in Paris and hundreds of thousands in Belgium and England, focused on his attributes of unspoiled American youth as a part of national pride. As Richard Oulahan pointed out at a National Press Club dinner in Washington, the press was to be congratulated for

bringing to the peoples of the world a new realization that clean living, clean thinking, fair play and sportsmanship, modesty of speech and manner, faith in a mother's prayers, have a front page news value intriguing imagination and inviting emulation, and are still potent as fundamentals of success.[6]

The personal tone of these remarks, stressing ideal moral character rather than the deed itself, was typical of the image-making that accompanied Lindbergh's achievements.

Unfortunately, their preoccupation with Lindbergh eventually produced a tension that grew into a kind of love-hate relationship. Newspaper coverage helped the aviator promote progress in aircraft development, airfields, and commercial travel, which were the major goals of his eighty-two-city tour in 1927 and his flights through Latin America in 1928. Reporters kept Charles constantly in the public eye, dutifully telling the people of his flights and on-time arrivals, his long solo hops across the Gulf of Mexico, and his records for speed and safety. But these technical, repetitive details did not satisfy their hunger for personal information, especially concerning Lindbergh's romantic interests or other private activities. Consequently, writers began to note every smile or gracious word he directed toward young women, and they had a field day with his courtship of, and eventual marriage to, Anne Morrow. In fact, after their wedding, a number of overly zealous reporters pursued the newlyweds to the harbor, where they intended to embark on a honeymoon cruise. They circled the Lindberghs' launch, blowing whistles and flashing lights, until they induced the couple to come on deck for pictures. Each similar incident led Charles to decry the media's influence on American society, but there is little doubt that his own influence would have been significantly reduced if it had not existed.

The darker side of this relationship emerged, however, with the kidnapping of Charles, Jr., in 1932. Again, the Lindberghs were the center of massive press coverage. To be sure, many of the reports were sympathetic and restrained, and one good result of the public interest that developed from media attention was that kidnapping became a serious issue. In fact, largely because it involved such beloved public figures, this case led to a new federal law establishing kidnapping as a capital crime. But a number of reporters seemed to delight in presenting to the public the most unsavory details of the crime and the ensuing trial of Bruno Richard Hauptmann. Letters and telegrams, many of them abusive and cruel, poured in to the Lindberghs again, and the family found it impossible to live without intrusions. When photographers eventually tried to break into a New Jersey morgue for pictures of the dead child and others ran a car carrying Jon Lindbergh off the road for more pictures of the Lindberghs' second-born, Charles determined to seek refuge from the more prurient aspects of American culture by leaving for England. Lauren Lyman's story of their travail in the December 23, 1935, *New York Times*, which won the Pulitzer Prize for journalism, reviewed the three-and-one-half-year saga of crime, conviction, and harassment and noted the sad part played by an unruly press. Just as the media had turned Lindbergh's private battle with the elements over the Atlantic into a heroic victory, their coverage of the kidnapping turned it into public tragedy and, finally, public castigation.

A third event in Lindbergh's life also played out through the media—his stand against American intervention in World War II. He decided to speak out, despite being aware that this decision would vault him once more into the news, because he was committed to stopping what appeared to be an inevitable movement toward war. Just as his flight had crystallized national pride, his speeches against intervention energized public debate on aid to the Allies and its relationship to actual conflict. Again, radio and the newspapers made such debate possible. In large arenas, such as Madison Square Garden or the Hollywood Bowl, Charles addressed thousands of people on the issues, but his radio broadcasts and news accounts of his speeches carried the most impact. For example, after his infamous address at Des Moines, in which he blamed the Roosevelt administration, the press, and the Jews for driving America toward war, headlines screamed these comments across the nation. Several pamphlets, issued by Anti-Defamation Councils or Defense Leagues, include more than 120 pages of news clippings impugning his remarks and calling for a public apology. These vituperative replies, most claiming that Lindbergh's address demonstrated his Nazi sympathies and bigotry once and for all, doubled the circulation of many newspapers during the following weeks before Pearl Harbor.

When the Japanese attack on Hawaii signaled America's entry into the war, it also marked the end of Lindbergh's significant influence on public opinion. Although he was to have a major effect on the war effort and on post-war aviation, he was never again so completely in the national arena. Yet, the image of him reflected in print is so strong that people who know of him at all generally recall either his transatlantic flight or his "Nazi sympathies" during World War II. He is in many ways the first, and may be still the greatest, media figure in the twentieth century.

PHOTOGRAPHS, FILMS, FILM STRIPS, AND RECORDINGS

Another dimension of Lindbergh's place in popular culture is the way his flights and other activities have been translated into visual forms. Francis T. Miller estimated that more than 50,000 photographs had been taken of him by 1929, and his own publication of Lindbergh's story in pictures contained 372 items from sixty-five nations and states.[7] Since then, the aviator's portrait has appeared, often on the cover, in every major American news magazine. It would be impossible to estimate how many additional photographs reside in private collections—of friends as well as complete strangers who snapped a picture as a souvenir of having been near enough to secure one.

Even more significant to Lindbergh's effect on mass culture was the motion picture film. For example, William Fox inaugurated the Movietone News just a month before Lindbergh's transatlantic flight, so crews were able to film his departure from Roosevelt Field and arrival at Le Bourget, as well as his tickertape parade up New York's Broadway and

President Coolidge's welcome at the White House. James H. Farmer notes that Charles's voice on Movietone "produced box office crowds comparable to those attracted in more recent years to the likes of *Jaws* or *Star Wars.*"[8] Movietone patrons at New York's Roxie Theater stood and cheered the premier Lindbergh footage uproariously for ten minutes, and the entire June 1927 issue of Movietone was devoted to Lindbergh's epic flight.

Besides this direct use of Lindbergh's feat, moviemakers often drew from it to inspire other flying films or to dedicate these films to Lindbergh in the advertisements. Nearly any mention of the transatlantic flight was enough to encourage patronage. For example, director William Wellman's famous production of *Wings*, completed for Paramount just three months after Charles's flight, was dedicated to him and to other "young warriors of the sky, whose wings were forever folded." Even Walt Disney used a Lindbergh poster to inspire Mickey and Minnie Mouse to fly in an airborne barnyard classic called *Plane Crazy* (1928). And nicknames, such as "The Flying Fool" or "The Lone Eagle," offered ready-made titles for a rash of screen offerings in 1927 and 1928.

Most of these early films appealed to the popular taste for comedy rather than to a sense of accuracy or history. For example, in *Flying Luck* (1927), comedy star Monty Banks and Jean Arthur reenact some of the aviator's experiences as a military cadet at Brooks AFB. With a nonexistent love interest thrown in for public appeal, the film emphasizes aerial stunting and near crashes similar to those described in Lindbergh's *We*. Fox Films' *Publicity Madness* (1927) simply uses headlines and segments of Charles's flight to launch its story line. In this comedy starring Edmund Lowe and Lois Moran, the hero intends to fly the Atlantic Ocean to prove his worth but chooses a Pacific flight instead after Charles lands at Le Bourget. Other films, such as *A Hero for a Night* (1927) or *Flying Romeos* (1928) are even more tenuously connected to the real event. The former stars screen comedian Glenn Tryon as Hiram Hastings, a taxi driver who wants to be a transatlantic flyer. Except for his ordinary background and rustic name, very likely used to suggest that anyone can fly who puts his mind to it, little else involves Lindbergh or his life. The latter stars the comedy team of Sidney and Murray, posing as a pair of barbers who become would-be transoceanic fliers. Most of this film is occupied with predictable scenes of aerial stunting— in an aircraft called "The Spirit of Goldberg." The preponderance of comedies in this list of titles is understandable. Few could relate to the "heroic" proportions of Lindbergh's flight, but all could find the humor in his rise from farm boy to flyer, especially in a machine that was still the butt of jokes and derision. These films reflect an interesting popular view of flying as a kind of stunt, the very view that Lindbergh had to overcome to make commercial aviation viable in the United States.

Various aspects of Lindbergh's career inform a number of more serious films, filmstrips, and recordings, many of which continue to be used for television or in classrooms. These, too, have influenced popular culture by preserving his feats in the minds of succeeding generations. For example, *American and Foreign Wars*, a series of audio tapes produced for Radio Yesteryear in 1965, contains six of Lindbergh's vital speeches against American intervention in World War II. *General Charles Lindbergh: the Wisdom of Wilderness* (1969) is a filmstrip, with an accompanying phonodisc recording Lindbergh's narration, which presents his views on conservation. Other brief documentaries, loop films, and black-and-white shorts usually summarize main events of his life. Most interesting of the 8mm or 16mm educational films are two by Wolper Productions, released in 1962 and 1964, respectively. The first, simply titled *Charles Lindbergh*, is a black-and-white, 16mm, sound biography that lasts about thirty minutes. The second, called *Lindbergh versus the Atlantic*, is similar in type and length. It compiles numerous authentic original films to present the story of Lindbergh and his solo transatlantic flight. Both were released during the time when he had become active in conservation issues, sparking renewed interest in who he was and what he had done.

Feature-length films have been made on two key events of Lindbergh's life: the Atlantic flight and the kidnapping of Charles, Jr. The first is Billy Wilder's production of *The Spirit of St. Louis* (1957), which is based on the Pulitzer Prize-winning autobiography of the same name. With Jimmy Stewart in the title role, the film achieved critical acclaim but mediocre box-office success. Although some critics speculated that Stewart's age made his portrayal of a twenty-five-year-old Charles unbelievable, the truth was that many moviegoers did not know who the hero was. After all, readers of autobiography are often not patrons of the movies. Still, the film is a perennial favorite as a family movie for small gatherings, and its production values make it the most entertaining source of information about Lindbergh.

Less entertaining, and considerably more biased in its portrayal of the aviator, is Buzz Kulik and Columbia Pictures Television's *The Lindbergh Kidnapping Case* (1976). The interesting thing about this film (and its recent renewals on late-night television) is that it parallels a continuing fascination with the case in books and newspaper articles. New Jersey's decision to reopen the investigation, at the insistence of Bruno Hauptmann's widow, has fueled speculation that Hauptmann was innocent. If this were so, Lindbergh's testimony at the trial and his identification of Hauptmann's voice as that of the person who claimed the ransom money would be suspect. The film, in fact, presents Charles as a vindictive, utterly possessed soul, who falsely condemns an innocent man to his death. Probably based on Andrew K. Dutch's *Hysteria* (1975) or Anthony Scaduto's *Scapegoat* (1976), which present similar theses, the film's bias and melodramatic rendering transmit a bizarre view of Lindbergh to a generation removed more than fifty years from the actual events. But it does show how Lindbergh's image and life continue to linger in American culture.

MUSICAL COMPOSITIONS, SONGS, POEMS, AND MEMORABILIA

Besides the flood of newsprint journalism and other media forms, Lindbergh's career inspired hundreds of creative works, ranging from symphonies and popular songs to poetry and sculpture. The three events that appear most frequently are the transatlantic flight, the birth of the Lindberghs' first child, and the kidnapping and death of that same child just two years later. Musical compositions, for example, were written from Los Angeles to Pittsburgh and from Klamath Falls, Oregon, to Muleshoe, Texas—some by rather well-known composers and songwriters. The most popular forms of published and unpublished titles were the march and the fox trot or waltz, showing that Lindbergh's life became a subject for cotillions and cavalcades, as well as dance halls and the musical stage.

Although choral and orchestral pieces aren't frequent, three deserve special mention. Radie Britain, who had already acquired a reputation for prize-winning choral compositions, wrote her *Heroic Poem* (1929) for orchestration to commemorate Lindbergh's transatlantic flight.[9] Bertolt Brecht, most famous for several modern dramas, collaborated with equally well-known composer Kurt Weill on a libretto for an operetta, entitled *The Flight of the Lindberghs*, in 1930. It takes as its subject the courtship and marriage of Charles and Anne Morrow, a "flight" of emotions especially suited to this light-hearted form. Finally, Harl McDonald composed a choral work, *Lament for the Stolen* (1938), incorporating several events from the kidnapping of the Lindbergh baby. It's a sympathetic rendering, which blends elements of the classical elegy with contemporary description. None of these works was widely popular, of course, but all were performed in New York. Brecht and Weill's operetta also appeared on the musical stage in Berlin. To some degree, then, they add to public awareness of Charles's joys and sorrows.

The marches draw their titles from Lindbergh's name, his nicknames—such as Lindy or the Lone Eagle—or his plane. Their words emphasize his pluck, courage, modesty, service to country, and love or concern for his mother. Howard Johnson and Al Sherman's "Lindbergh (the Eagle of the U.S.A.)" is typical in many ways. On the sheet music, published by Shapiro and Bernstein in 1927, there are pictures of Charles and his mother, whose wondrous love and prayers were presumed to provide the strength upon which his success rested. The march rhythms are appropriately stirring for a noble subject, and the words stress his flying alone against fate and unknown dangers to gain his place in history. Other marches are paeans to triumphal Lindy, Lindbergh above the clouds, the *Spirit of St. Louis*, or "We"—Lindbergh's own name for himself and his airplane. Their lyrics call for praise, love, and homage to the brave lad who brought glory and honor to America, thus reflecting the public view of him as a regenerative force in American society.

This force is most apparent in the hundreds of popular songs and news-print poems that appeared in 1927 and 1928. Besides being published as sheet music, a number of the songs were recorded by well-known singers or presented as parts of Broadway musicals, thus adding to their effect on the public. For example, such fox trot songs as "Lucky Lindy," written by Abel Baer and L. Wolfe Gilbert; or "I Can't Give You Anything but Love, Lindy," by Dorothy Fields and Jimmy McHugh; or "Lindy, Lindy!" by Dok Eisenbourg were recorded for Columbia Records by Vernon Dalhart, Johnny Hamp, The Knickerbockers, Grey Gull, and other popular recording artists of the day. Waltzes such as "Like an Angel You Flew into Everyone's Heart," by McHugh and Harry Stone, or "I Owe It All to You (Mother O'Mine)," by McHugh and Irving Mills, take up the more sentimental aspects of the transatlantic flight—Mrs. Lindbergh's prayers, careful teaching, and love for her son being the primary subjects. Almost as inspired by the flight as McHugh, George M. Cohan wrote "When Lindy Comes Home" to commemorate it and respectfully dedicated his 1928 reissue of "The Yankee Doodle Boy" to Captain Charles A. Lindbergh. Finally, the aviator and his feat created one of the most popular dances of the late 1920s—the Lindy, or Lindy Hop—which eventually was transformed into the jitterbug of the 1930s and 1940s.

Equally remarkable was the outpouring of more than 2,000 published poems, most of which appeared in *Literary Digest* or *Poetry* magazine, in newspapers, or in edited collections. Many poems compare Lindbergh to explorers like Cortez or Columbus, to mythical types like Mercury or Apollo, or to literary figures like Lochinvar. Others attempt to capture his simplicity and American qualities in titles such as "Slim," "Our Boy," "Flying Fool," or "Pioneer of the Air." Nearly all emphasize his youth, courage, and vision, whereas some honor the magnificence of the machine in which he rode. Most of these lyrics are now buried, often deservedly, in newspaper files and microfilm collections, but they were widely read at the time. A few, such as Harriet Monroe's "To Lindbergh Flying"—in the March 1928 volume of *Poetry*—or Rostand's French lyric, "À Lindbergh," published in the June 1927 *Literary Digest*, have real literary merit. Fortunately, Arthur Hooley has collected 100 of the better efforts in *The Spirit of St. Louis* (1927). And the American search for heroes in the 1970s helped revive the Lindbergh legend in verse, at least temporarily. George G. Cox's *Lindbergh: An American Epic* and David Penhale's *New York to Paris*, both published in 1975, show that Lindbergh's spirit and accomplishment were still poetically alive nearly fifty years after he touched down at Le Bourget.

A final indicator of Lindbergh's influence is the massive number of medals, decorations, trophies, sculptures, medallions, decorative tapestries, ceramic plates, coins, and stamps that were produced to commemorate his achievement. Many thousands of popular medallions were sold soon after the transatlantic flight, for example, and beacons, airports, streets, and entire towns were named after him. Commemorative exhibits or sites still exist at the Smithsonian's National Air and Space Museum in Washington, D.C., the Jefferson Memorial in St. Louis, Lindbergh Field in San Diego, the Gimbel Room at the United States Air Force Academy, and the Lindbergh Historic Site in Little Falls, Minnesota. Each year, more than 2 million people see these exhibits, and thousands of copies of Lindbergh's *Spirit of St. Louis* or other books concerning his life continue to be sold.

It is impossible to assess precisely Lindbergh's effect on American popular culture in the twentieth century. The records of his popularity noted in this chapter merely skim the surface, for many people keep their memories of him only in their minds. When one mentions his name in a gathering, it isn't unusual to hear someone say that a mother, father, uncle, or friend of the family knew him—or at least, saw and admired him—from nearly every part of the country. He has served as hero, tragic victim, leader in public affairs, object of derision and calumny, conservator of natural beauty, and elder statesman. Most of all, he has been a touchstone of public emotions. Reflecting the pride, joy, certainty, sorrow, and faith of the nation, he has carved out an indelible place in its history.

NOTES

1. Sir Samuel Hoare, as quoted in Fitzhugh Green, "A Little of What the World Thought of Lindbergh," in Charles A. Lindbergh, *We* (New York: Grosset and Dunlap, 1927), pp. 259-260.

2. James Walker, as quoted in Green, "World Thought," p. 303.

3. Calvin Coolidge, as quoted in Green, "World Thought," p. 278.

4. Green, "World Thought," pp. 300-301.

5. A. M. Hughes, as quoted in Green, "World Thought," pp. 311-312.

6. Richard Oulahan, as quoted in Green, "World Thought," p. 285.

7. Francis T. Miller, *Lindbergh: His Story in Pictures* (New York: G. P. Putnam's Sons, 1929), pp. 1-10.

8. James H. Farmer, *Celluloid Wings* (Blue Ridge Summit, Pennsylvania: TAB Books, Inc., 1984), p. 74. Discussion of several of the following films depends on this source.

9. Some of the discussion in the next three paragraphs depends upon Roger D. Kinkle, *The Complete Encyclopedia of Pop Music and Jazz, 1900-1950* (New Rochelle, New York: Arlington House, 1974), for 1927 and 1928; and Edward Jablonski, *The Encyclopedia of American Music* (Garden City, New York: Doubleday, 1981), pp. 227, 258-260, and 341. I have also looked at twenty-five songs in sheet music at the Gimbel Collection of the United States Air Force Academy.

Lindbergh next to his DH-4 mail plane, used to fly the mail from St. Louis to Chicago for Robertson Aircraft Corporation in 1926. *National Air and Space Museum, Smithsonian Institution.*

Lindbergh before the *Spirit of St. Louis* at Roosevelt Field a few days before his flight. *National Air and Space Museum, Smithsonian Institution.*

THE "SPIRIT OF ST. LOUIS" AIRCRAFT

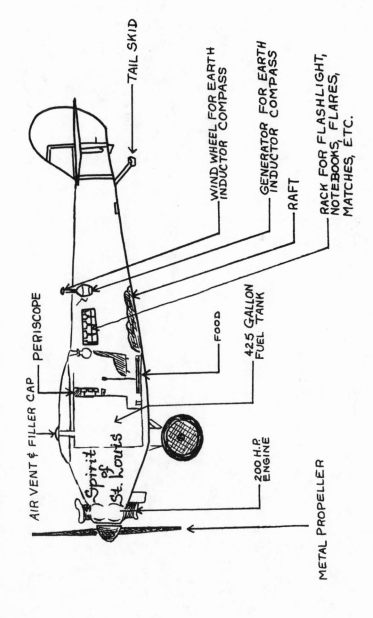

TAIL SKID

WIND WHEEL FOR EARTH
INDUCTOR COMPASS

GENERATOR FOR EARTH
INDUCTOR COMPASS

RAFT

RACK FOR FLASHLIGHT,
NOTEBOOKS, FLARES,
MATCHES, ETC.

PERISCOPE

AIR VENT & FILLER CAP

FOOD

425 GALLON
FUEL TANK

Spirit of St. Louis

200 H.P.
ENGINE

METAL PROPELLER

TRANSATLANTIC FLIGHT

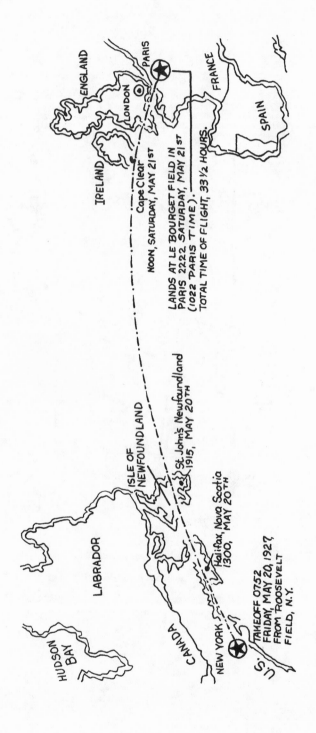

HUDSON BAY

LABRADOR

CANADA

ISLE OF NEWFOUNDLAND

St. John's Newfoundland 1915, MAY 20TH

Halifax, Nova Scotia 1300, MAY 20TH

NEW YORK

U.S. TAKEOFF 0752 FRIDAY, MAY 20, 1927, FROM ROOSEVELT FIELD, N.Y.

IRELAND

ENGLAND

LONDON

Cape Clear NOON, SATURDAY, MAY 21ST

PARIS

FRANCE

SPAIN

LANDS AT LE BOURGET FIELD IN PARIS 2222 SATURDAY, MAY 21ST (1022 PARIS TIME). TOTAL TIME OF FLIGHT, 33½ HOURS.

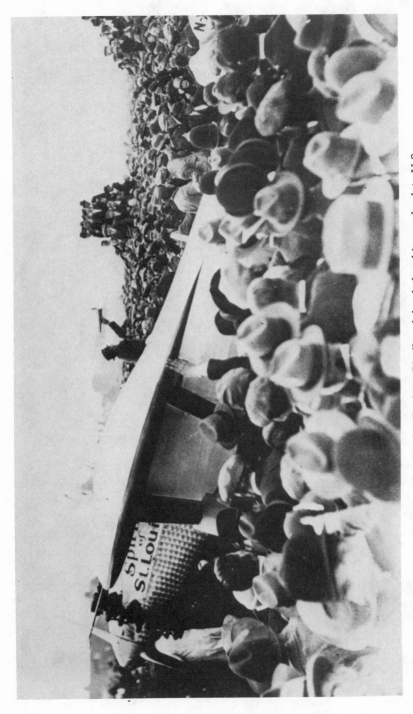

Crowd around *Spirit of St. Louis* at Croyden, England, where Lindbergh landed on his way back to U.S. on the *Memphis. National Air and Space Museum, Smithsonian Institution.*

Broadway honors Lindbergh's return from transatlantic flight, 1927. Crowds were estimated at 10 million. *National Air and Space Museum, Smithsonian Institution.*

UNITED STATES TOUR OF 48 STATES, 1927

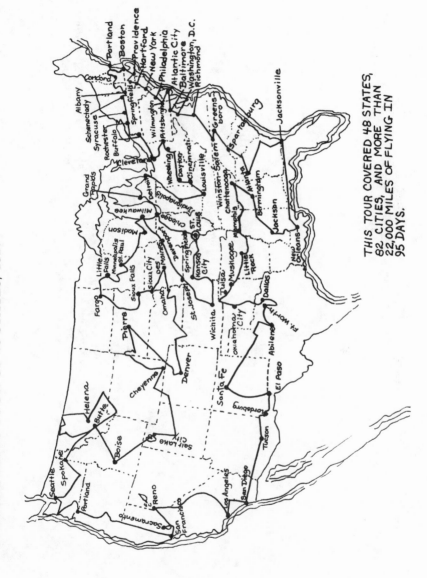

THIS TOUR COVERED 48 STATES,
82 CITIES, AND MORE THAN
22,000 MILES OF FLYING IN
95 DAYS.

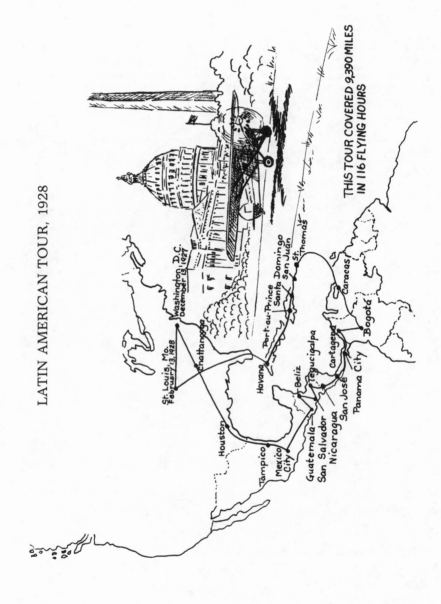

LATIN AMERICAN TOUR, 1928

THIS TOUR COVERED 9,390 MILES IN 116 FLYING HOURS

Washington, D.C.
December 13, 1927

St. Louis, Mo.
February 13, 1928

Chattanooga

Houston

Tampico

Mexico City

Guatemala
San Salvador
Nicaragua
San José

Beliz

Havana

Port-au-Prince

Tegucigalpa

Cartagena

Panama City

Bogotá

Santa Domingo
San Juan

St. Thomas

Caracas

Charles and Anne Lindbergh before their Lockheed *Sirius*, preparing to take off on 1931 exploratory flight over the polar cap to the Orient. *National Air and Space Museum, Smithsonian Institution.*

POLAR FLIGHT TO THE ORIENT, 1931

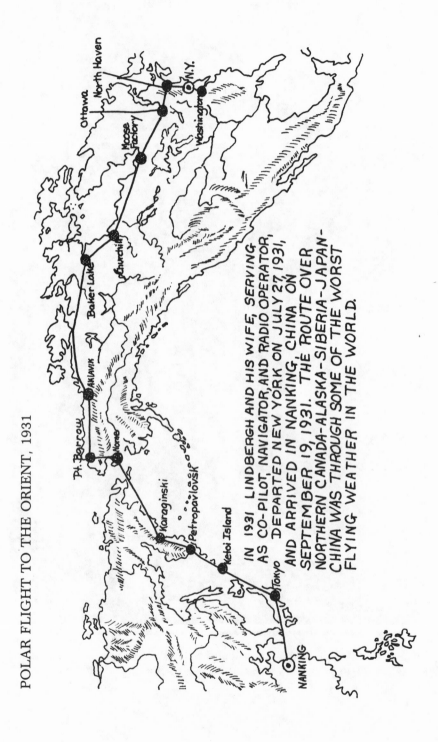

IN 1931 LINDBERGH AND HIS WIFE, SERVING AS CO-PILOT, NAVIGATOR, AND RADIO OPERATOR, DEPARTED NEW YORK ON JULY 27, 1931, AND ARRIVED IN NANKING, CHINA ON SEPTEMBER 19, 1931. THE ROUTE OVER NORTHERN CANADA-ALASKA-SIBERIA-JAPAN-CHINA WAS THROUGH SOME OF THE WORST FLYING WEATHER IN THE WORLD.

Lindbergh composite photograph. At center is famous "visionary" face, taken just before his trans- atlantic flight. *National Air and Space Museum, Smithsonian Institution.*

TRANSATLANTIC AIR ROUTE, 1933

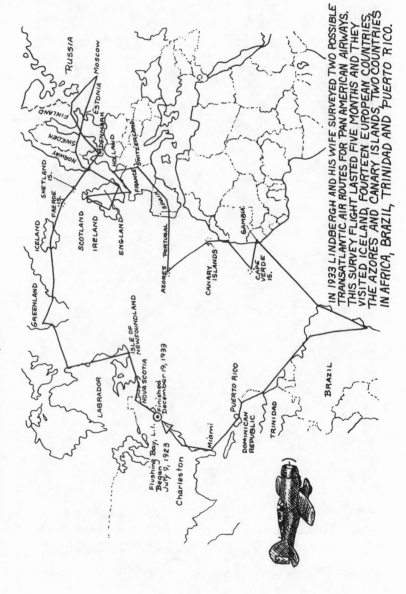

IN 1933 LINDBERGH AND HIS WIFE SURVEYED TWO POSSIBLE
TRANSATLANTIC AIR ROUTES FOR PAN AMERICAN AIRWAYS.
THIS SURVEY FLIGHT LASTED FIVE MONTHS AND THEY
VISITED ICELAND, FOURTEEN EUROPEAN COUNTRIES,
THE AZORES AND CANARY ISLANDS, TWO COUNTRIES
IN AFRICA, BRAZIL, TRINIDAD AND PUERTO RICO.

RUSSIA
MOSCOW
FINLAND
ESTONIA
SWEDEN
DENMARK
NORWAY
HOLLAND
SHETLAND IS.
FAEROE IS.
SCOTLAND
IRELAND
ICELAND
ENGLAND
FRANCE
SWITZERLAND
SPAIN
PORTUGAL
AZORES
CANARY ISLANDS
GAMBIA
CAPE VERDE IS.
GREENLAND
LABRADOR
ISLE OF NEWFOUNDLAND
NOVA SCOTIA
Finished December 19, 1933
Flushing Bay, L.I. Began July 9, 1923
Charleston
Miami
PUERTO RICO
DOMINICAN REPUBLIC
TRINIDAD
BRAZIL

Lindbergh with Major Joe Foss at Emirau Island in the South Pacific, 1944.
Courtesy of John Stanaway and the Lindbergh Historic Site, Little Falls, Minnesota.

Charles Lindbergh with Tommy McGuire in the South Pacific, summer of 1944.
Courtesy of John Stanaway and the Lindbergh Historic Site, Little Falls, Minnesota.

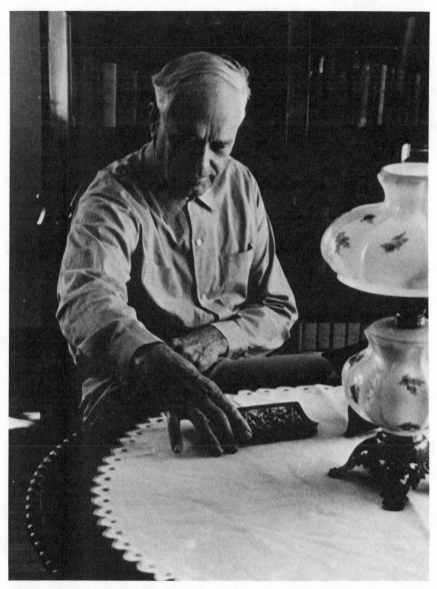

Lindbergh at his mother's dining room table, Lindbergh Historic Site, Little Falls, Minnesota, 1971. *Photograph by John Ferguson.*

4

LINDBERGH IN PRINT:
A BIBLIOGRAPHICAL ESSAY

Writings by and about Charles Lindbergh fall naturally into several categories that provide a ready framework for bibliographical description. But volume of material and a desire to choose only the most significant treatments of the Lindbergh story make this essay a task of selection. Thus, it locates major collections of Lindbergh materials, describes the aviator's own writings in functional groups, and briefly analyzes the most important books, chapters, or essays on his life and career in aviation. Most newspaper pieces and articles on peripheral matters do not appear here. A more thorough but by no means all-inclusive checklist is in the next chapter.

COLLECTIONS

With the exception of small collections of memorabilia in private hands, and a limited selection of sheet music and nonprint items at the U.S. Air Force Academy, Lindbergh materials are in six major locations: the Sterling Memorial Library of Yale University, the Library of Congress, the Smithsonian Institution's National Air and Space Museum, the Missouri Historical Society Archives in St. Louis, the Special Collections branch of the Minnesota Historical Society in St. Paul, and the Lindbergh Historical Site at Little Falls, Minnesota. Each collection has unique features, as well as some duplication of items found elsewhere.

Yale University is by far the largest source of written, printed, and photographic documents on the Lindberghs. After his transatlantic flight, Charles began to cart boxes of letters, drafts and typescripts of speeches or articles, copies of newspaper clippings, photographs, published books and articles, and many other materials to the Yale Library—knowing that he was preserving at least one small part of America's history, in addition to his own. The library now has more than 300 linear feet of Lindbergh papers, with access severely restricted to those who obtain special permission from the family—through their literary executor, William Jovanovich, of Harcourt Brace Jovanovich.

The Library of Congress holds several hundred items, including published biographies, histories of aviation in which Lindbergh appears, approximately one dozen books on Charles, Jr.'s, kidnapping and the Hauptmann trial, and numerous commemorative pamphlets. Records of presidential speeches in Lindbergh's honor, two books of poems concerning the transatlantic flight, and other miscellaneous items round out the printed collection and records in the Office of Copyrights. These two sources provide an extensive list of songs, compositions, recordings, and films, together with a few actual scores and music sheets, that have helped create the Lindbergh legend. All are open to researchers.

Far less extensive are the Smithsonian's archives. Available to researchers in the library of the Air and Space Museum are several folders, which contain clippings, photocopies of salient articles on Lindbergh's career, informal bibliographical lists, and photographs. Of course, the museum also houses an essential partner to Lindbergh's fame—the *Spirit of St. Louis*—suspended from its main gallery ceiling. A few original artifacts from the famous flight top off this visual display.

Some 15,000 separate items, many inaccessible, make up the collection of memorabilia at the Missouri Historical Society's Jefferson Memorial in St. Louis. A selective catalog of the collection was published in 1977 by the society, but it only begins to show the range and depth of public feeling toward Lindbergh's transatlantic flight and other achievements in aviation. All of the official awards are here: the Congressional Medal of Honor; the Special Medal of Congress; the Hubbard, Langley, Harmon, and Wright Brothers Memorial Trophies; the French Legion of Honor. Engraved medallions, cups, silver and gold crosses, busts, desk sets, jewel boxes, vases, keys to cities, and many other commemorative awards from private citizens, governments, and aviation clubs or societies all testify to Lindbergh's impact on the world. A number are on permanent display at the Jefferson Memorial building.

The Minnesota Historical Society and Lindbergh Historic Site at Little Falls contain some unique materials. Original scrapbooks compiled by Minnesota residents, files of local and regional new stories, and historical information on Little Falls are some of the special items one can find at the Historical Society's library. The Lindbergh Site and Interpretive Center has attractive displays and a completely restored homesite. All the details of Lindbergh's early biography come to life here: "Moo Pond," a suspension bridge, a screened porch where Charles first dreamed of flying, Mrs. Lindbergh's books and china, Saxon Six and Volkswagen automobiles used by the young farm boy and middle-aged aviator, and the beauties of nature along the upper Mississippi. Some correspondence and oral histories involving Lindbergh's boyhood friends and neighbors are also in the center's files and are accessible to serious scholars.

LINDBERGH'S WRITINGS

Lindbergh wrote works of three kinds: autobiography; articles or speeches on aviation, medicine, politics, or conservation; and forewords for a few books, usually written by or about friends.

Autobiographies

The autobiographies reveal a maturing mind responding to an increasingly complex environment. His fledgling descriptions of airplane accidents or parachute jumps are journeyman accounts—terse, unornamented narratives. *We*, a recounting of events leading up to his landing at Le Bourget in France, is a similarly spare 30,000 words. Written in 1927 under pressure of a twenty-day deadline, it fills in some information on his family and background and then concentrates on his efforts to fly the Atlantic: his original idea on a mail flight from St. Louis to Chicago, attempts to secure backing and to procure his monoplane, and the flights from San Diego to St. Louis to New York to Paris.

Once Charles and Anne were married, she took over the job as chronicler of their adventures, so no biographical writing from his pen found its way to print until after World War II. Meantime, during the 1930s, he experienced deep sorrow over the death of his baby boy and anger against the press and public. His anti-intervention stance before the war further sharpened his political and philosophical insights, and the atrocities of war colored his view of technology and human life. Thus, by the time he published *Of Flight and Life* in 1948, his thinking and writing had become more introspective, more carefully wrought. In fact, the essay on his near death in a P-47 combines the best qualities of what would become a prize-winning style: terse, fast-paced action balanced by sharp description and thoughtful observation. His *The Wartime Journals of Charles A. Lindbergh*, though not published until 1970, actually belong to this period as well. They are a fascinating account of his life in Europe during the late 1930s, his work to alert people to the dangers of impending conflict, the busy rounds of speeches to argue for nonintervention, and his own combat experiences in the South Pacific. In his descriptions—of beauty, courage, pain, and degradation—Charles shows unusual ability.

When *The Spirit of St. Louis* appeared in 1953, it deserved the acclaim it won and its best-seller status. Lindbergh's technique had advanced remarkably. The exciting present-tense narrative of his transatlantic flight merges smoothly with associative flashbacks to his past and philosophical musing on reality, courage, mental awareness, and ghostly spirits. The result fully captures the experience of a solo transatlantic crossing, so a reader can understand what endurance flights require of the pilot. For achieving a work of "high literary merit," Lindbergh received the Pulitzer Prize for biography in May 1954.

Other than scattered forewords and occasional articles revealing his association with Robert Goddard, Alexis Carrel, astronaut Michael Collins, and various conservation groups, Lindbergh wrote just two other autobiographical works. *Boyhood on the Upper Mississippi* is a reminiscent letter, composed in installments written from all over the world during 1972. With remarkable accuracy for a seventy-year-old man, Charles traces his early life in Little Falls up to his departure for the University of Wisconsin in 1920. This slim book is nicely bound and illustrated, with an introduction by Russell Fridley, of the Minnesota Historical Society, detailing events leading to the dedication of the Lindbergh homestead as a state park.

Lindbergh's last book, *An Autobiography of Values*, was in manuscript when he died in 1974. Judith Schiff, of the Yale Library's special collections branch, and publisher William Jovanovich edited the more than 1,000 pages into a final form that reflects the author's deepening concern for the future of civilization and his own place in its progress. Rather than simply rehashing events, Lindbergh instead returns to memories that helped form his values and tries to assess how those values have held up over a lifetime. The work as it is published becomes a mature capstone to a life of activity and service to country.

As Lindbergh has observed, all autobiography is a product of focus and exclusion. The writer casts his light upon certain details and leaves others in shadow. His own books reflect a continual reevaluation of his place in the universe—from man of action, to analyst and commentator on the actions of a nation, to admirer of the enduring spiritual qualities of the natural world. They remain the most accurate and valuable revelations of his life and mind.

Aviation, Science, Politics, and Conservation

Lindbergh's articles on aviation and medicine are generally technical accounts, written in straightforward, objective prose. They are of interest because they reflect the range of his expertise. Sikorsky, the well-known airplane designer, said that Lindbergh's true value lay in his ability to test a plane and then come to the drawing board and help redesign it. His pre-World War II letters and intelligence estimates on German air power illustrate how well he understood aircraft design and production. Testimony before congressional committees, such as his

"Statement on Air Corps Expansion Program" in 1940, also displays his knowledge of aircraft specifications and design possibilities.

Perhaps most surprising to those who do not know the details of Lindbergh's life outside aviation is the discovery of his scientific writings. Besides many journal and laboratory notebook accounts of high-altitude tests and other physiological experiments, he published a series of articles on the perfusion of whole organs for surgical operations. After meeting surgeon Alexis Carrel and discovering that no apparatus existed to allow doctors to keep organs alive outside the body, he set his mind to solving the problem. In 1931 and 1932, he wrote two articles for *Science* magazine that describe his "Apparatus to Circulate Liquid Under Constant Pressure in a Closed System" and his "Method for Washing Corpuscles in Suspension." Four years later, he had developed a more advanced version of the apparatus and discovered several other devices that would become useful in organ transplant surgery. Articles in *The Journal of Experimental Medicine* and coauthorship of *The Culture of Organs*, with Alexis Carrel, resulted from this work at the Rockefeller Institute. Although he stopped working on his perfusion apparatus after 1939, new research revived it in 1966, when investigators found that it could be used in combination with deep-freezing of organs for transplants. His article in *Cryobiology*, "An Apparatus for the Pulsating Perfusion of Whole Organs," documents his part in these investigations.

A scan of Lindbergh's publications reveals a clustering of his interests around certain causes or problems. For example, nonintervention in World War II and conservation dominate his list of published speeches and articles from 1939 to 1974. His first speech against joining the war in Europe, called "Appeal for Isolation," appeared in the October 1939 issue of *Vital Speeches of the Day*. In all, sixteen of his public talks appeared in *Vital Speeches* or *Scribner's Commentator* between October 1939 and November 1941. Five especially vital ones are batched in *The Radio Addresses of Charles A. Lindbergh*, published by Scribner's in 1940, and his main ideas are summarized in "Lindbergh for the Record: Views on the Great Controversial Issues of the Day." *Scribner's Commentator*, 10 (August 1941):7-13. Together with articles in *Reader's Digest*, *Atlantic Monthly*, and *Collier's*, as well as his *Wartime Journals*, these transcripts of speeches are an important record of Lindbergh's noninterventionist views.

Articles on conservation issues appear in earnest beginning in 1964, but Charles had begun to talk about the "quality of life" fifteen years before that. His acceptance speech for the Wright Brothers Memorial Trophy in 1949 stressed the need to balance the hot-house atmosphere of scientific progress with human qualities, including the appreciation of nature and culture. His "The Fourth Dimension of Survival" (*Saturday Review*, 1954) and "Our Best Chance to Survive" (*Saturday Evening Post*, 1954) expand upon this theme, pointing out that technology may obliterate man's natural connections with the earth. But it is not until ten years later that he has moved to conservation as the primary way of bolstering essential values. He sounds this approach clearly in "Is Civilization Progress?"—an essay written for *Reader's Digest* in 1964. Over the next ten years, seven more articles for the *Digest* and *Life* magazine stress the "wisdom of wildness" and "lessons from the primitive." To young people of the 1960s, in fact, Lindbergh was a very different sort of hero—a member of the old guard fervently joining a cause to protect the future.

Forewords and Prefaces

Lindbergh's forewords and prefaces begin with his notes on an article Anne did for *National Geographic* in 1934. Charles provided comments on navigation and flying, as well as flight maps, for "Flying Around the North Atlantic," which describes their survey trip of 29,000 miles in 1933. On this same excursion, he had taken air samples of plant spores and bacteria in the Arctic regions; his field notes became a part of F. C. Meier's "Collecting Microorganisms from the Arctic Atmosphere," published in the January 1935 issue of *Scientific Monthly*. Lindbergh's maps and notes appeared in Anne's book-length version of their northern trip—*North to the Orient* (1935)—and in her *Listen! The Wind* (1938), which reported their junket from the Cape Verde Islands to Natal, Brazil two years later.

People or issues he cared about fostered other introductory essays from 1950 to 1974. For example, his associations with Alexis Carrel, Robert Goddard, and John Grierson produced prefaces to *The Voyage to Lourdes* (1950), by Carrel, and *This High Man: The Life of Robert H. Goddard* (1963), by Milton Lehman. He also wrote forewords to Grierson's *Challenge to the Poles* (1964) and to *Alexis Carrel: Visionary Surgeon* (1971), by W. Stirling Edwards and Peter D. Edwards. His admiration and kinship for the brilliant but eccentric Carrel are particularly evident in his notes on their time spent together, both in America and in France. Finally, a biography of his father, *Lindbergh of Minnesota* (1973), by Bruce Larson, gave Charles a chance to remark on some of C. A.'s political activities, at which he often acted as driver and helper. Lindbergh's interest in space programs and conservation generated a few more short introductions during the last few years of his life. He wrote forewords to *Vanguard: A History* (1971), by Constance M. Green and Milton Lomask, and *Carrying the Fire: An Astronaut's Journey* (1974), by Michael Collins. The first tells of his contacts with American satellite developments; the second relates his involvement in space medicine and astronaut training during the early years of the Apollo program. Besides his introduction to *Maui: The Last Hawaiian Place* (1970), a conservationist book published by the Friends of the Earth Society, Lindbergh's last piece of finished writing was also on conservation and wilderness. Just five months before he died, he completed a foreword to *The Gentle Tasaday* (1975), by John Nance. It describes his efforts on behalf of the Tasaday people and expresses his belief that their primitive values held an important lesson for contemporary society: that progress is hollow if it obliterates the essential quality of life.

BIOGRAPHICAL BOOKS, CHAPTERS, AND ARTICLES

Materials written by others about Lindbergh include full-length biographies, diaries or memoirs on certain periods, chapters in books on aviation heroes or history, biographical articles in journals, and hundreds of newspaper accounts concerning almost every public detail of his life. In the selective discussion that follows, I have grouped these materials into several manageable categories, based on the major events or periods of Lindbergh's career.

General

Several full-length biographies exist, but none of them is an authorized account, written with full access to the Lindbergh papers. Until the authorized biography by Raymond Fredette appears (in progress as of this writing), readers must rely on several incomplete accounts. The early biographies, such as *Charles Lindbergh: His Life* (1927), by Dale Van Every and Norris Tracy, tend to be quickly assembled pieces—often compiled from newspaper stories and interviews. James H. Burden's *An Interpretation of Colonel Lindbergh's Achievements* (1928) or George Fife's *Lindbergh the Lone Eagle: His Life and Achievements* (1927) or Isaac Van Kampen's *Lindbergh: A Saga of Youth* (1928) are typical examples. A few boyhood stories combine with a bit of information about Lindbergh as a farmer, college student, daredevil barnstormer, and airmail pilot to form a brief background for the events leading up to his transatlantic flight. Most of the biography then concerns itself with the way Slim Lindbergh transformed himself into national hero by flying the Atlantic alone. Of course, these early efforts were aimed at getting news about Lindbergh out to the public as quickly as possible, not at giving careful analyses of his life and character.

Supplemental material appears in several specialized works. For example, Lindbergh's family background is covered in *The Lindberghs* (1931), by Lynn and Dora B. Haines, and in Bruce Larson's *Lindbergh of Minnesota* (1973). Don Dwiggins reviews the details of Lindbergh's barnstorming career in a part of *The Barnstormers: Flying Daredevils of the Roaring Twenties* (1968), and Donald Keyhoe tells what it was like to travel with him on the forty-eight-state tour of America in *Flying with Lindbergh* (1928). An interesting alternative to words on his early career is Francis Miller's *Lindbergh: His Story in Pictures* (1929), which nicely reflects his popularity as a photographic subject. Except for Anne M. Lindbergh's several volumes of diaries covering the years from 1928 to 1944, John Grierson's *I Remember Lindbergh* (1977) is the best of several personal reminiscences, all of which are limited by infrequent contact with their subject and the specialized perspective of friendship. This potpourri of works merely begins to reflect the vast number of articles and chapters written on various aspects of his long public career, but most of the essential information appears in more accessible book-length form.

The first book to incorporate a fuller range of events was *The Hero: Charles A. Lindbergh and the American Dream* (1959), by Kenneth S. Davis. It remains a valuable resource because of its thoroughness and its analysis of Lindbergh's career in light of American society. Davis draws upon hundreds of printed sources, as well as personal interviews, and he includes a lengthy bibliographical essay on these sources for serious researchers. Walter S. Ross benefitted from previous research and from the perspective of additional years when he wrote *The Last Hero: Charles A. Lindbergh* (Second Edition, 1976). It is the best single book on the aviator's life. His balanced approach to his subject allows him to point out Lindbergh's shortcomings while painting a positive picture of a remarkable human being. Interviews with friends and family members, who were less constrained from speaking after Lindbergh's death in 1974, improve the reader's understanding of the post-war period. And Ross's observations on the public man's family life, child-rearing philosophy, and friendships make Lindbergh more human, more accessible to those of us who did not know him.

Leonard Mosley's *Lindbergh: A Biography* (1976) is also a detailed, adeptly written study, useful for its additions to the work of Davis and Ross. It is marred, however, by its argumentative tone and overriding thesis. Mosley labors a bit too hard to reinterpret Lindbergh's life, to fight against seeing him as an American hero. In fact, his treatment of the noninterventionist years and of Lindbergh's associations with the Germans before World War II tries to represent Charles as self-righteous, sympathetic to Nazi views, and possibly responsible for Allied capitulation to Hitler at Munich. Other observations suggest that Charles was pathologically opposed to the press and to all liberal views. Combined with some errors in dates and events, as well as chapter titles in questionable taste—"The Fat Lamb Is Stolen" on the kidnapping and death of Charles, Jr., for example—Mosley's bias makes this book irritating to read.

Two collections of articles form an important supplement to Lindbergh's biography. The first is a group of four long essays "Commemorating the Twenty-fifth Anniversary of Lindbergh's New York-Paris Flight'' and published in the May 1952 number of *Aero Digest*. They describe Lindbergh's contributions to technical developments in aviation, from his advanced demands for the *Spirit of St. Louis* to his work on the B-24 bomber and various fighter aircraft of World War II. The second is *Charles A. Lindbergh: An American Life*, edited by Tom Crouch for the Smithsonian Institution. In this volume commemorating the fiftieth anniversary of the transatlantic flight, six essays describing Lindbergh's contributions to American society join an excellent checklist of Lindberghiana by Dominick Pisano, reference librarian at the National Air and Space Museum. These articles span the flier's career, from the barnstorming years to his interests in space and conservation.

The Transatlantic Flight

Although no one has told the tale of Lindbergh's Atlantic crossing as well as he does in *The Spirit of St. Louis*, good accounts appear in several longer works on aviation. Edward Jablonski's *Atlantic Fever* (1972) and Robert de la Croix's *They Flew the Atlantic* (1959) are two of the best. Both men capture the mounting excitement of the flight, as competitors positioned themselves near New York and prepared to leap out toward the ocean in a variety of flying machines. They describe how Lindbergh finally got off a muddy runway in the wee hours of the morning and then draw on Lindbergh's version of his flight to show the fatigue and danger of a long night journey. *Wings Over the Atlantic* (1956), by Robert Hoare, and *The Brave Men: Twelve Portraits of Courage* (1967), by Mark Sufrin, are equally descriptive, picking up small details of Lindbergh's flying regimen, noting how he slapped himself repeatedly to stay awake, and showing his jubilation upon reaching the coast of Ireland.

Accuracy of detail and authenticity are common to all four of these chapters, but the official account of Lindbergh's crossing appears in the State Department's *The Flight of Captain Charles A. Lindbergh from New York to Paris* (1927). It draws upon official records of time and position sightings along the route to outline precisely how the flight progressed. Together, these summaries recreate the experience of Lindbergh's daring challenge against the unknown.

The most exciting versions of Lindbergh's flight are not in aviation histories, however. Illustrated books for juvenile readers hold that honor. Here, the illustrator's art helps picture the tiny plane swallowed by a bleak sky, and the adventure writer's charged words hold the young reader of another generation in suspense over the flier's fate. *Dangerous Adventure! Lindbergh's Famous Flight* (1977), by Ruth Gross, and Nicholas Fisk's *Lindbergh the Lone Flier* (1968) are particularly good accounts, as are John T. Foster's *The Flight of the Lone Eagle* (1974) and Gerald

Kurland's *Lindbergh Flies the Atlantic* (1975). All rely on Lindbergh's autobiography for details of the flight, so they are reasonably accurate as well as engaging.

Equally interesting, though, are the reactions to Lindbergh's accomplishment. Publicity and enthusiasm welled up from all parts of the globe. As Fitzhugh Green documents in "A Little of What the World Thought of Lindbergh," published as part of Lindbergh's *We* (1927), thousands of gifts and congratulations flowed to the aviator. Millions of words appeared in print, attempting to recreate his feat in words for the news-hungry public.

In the following years, numerous commentators have tried to assess what the flight meant to aviation and to the American spirit. The best single article on the subject is John William Ward's "The Meaning of Lindbergh's Flight," published in a 1958 number of *American Quarterly*. He shows how Lindbergh's heroic act regenerated American pride in the lone pioneer while also justifying the country's headlong rush into technological progress. Without both, the crossing would have been impossible. Similar approaches are in Lowell Thomas's *Famous First Flights that Changed History* (1968), Dixon Wecter's *The Hero in America: A Chronicle of Hero Worship* (1941), and James K. Fitzpatrick's *Builders of the American Dream* (1977). Rounding out this list is Harry F. Guggenheim's "The Significance of Lindbergh's Flight," in *The Seven Skies* (1930). It demonstrates what the flight meant to commercial aviation, travel, and international business, all of which received a tremendous boost from its accompanying publicity.

Other Exploratory Flights and Commercial Aviation

Lindbergh knew that he had to capitalize on the immense impact of his transatlantic flight by transferring public enthusiasm to commercial aviation. His first step was to promote flying and airmail in the United States, so he joined Harry Guggenheim in planning a forty-eight-state tour. In Milton Lomask's *Seed Money: The Guggenheim Story* (1964) and Richard P. Hallion, Jr.'s, *Legacy of Flight: The Guggenheim Contribution to American Aviation* (1977), we learn just how successful the plan was. Lindbergh dropped promotional leaflets over many small towns and landed at eighty-two cities enroute, missing his assigned landing time only once—because of fog on the runway. Hallion and Lomask point out the huge increase in painted navigational aids and markings, airfields, lights, and actual pounds of mail carried by air that resulted from Lindbergh's timely advertisements.

The more personal side of this tour emerges in Donald Keyhoe's *Flying with Lindbergh* (1928). Keyhoe, a Department of Commerce representative on the flight, usually flew with Phil Love in a lead plane, but he saw

Charles in many informal situations. Thus, he could convey the practical joker and pilot, as well as the "serious man of public events." People who recall seeing Lindbergh on the tour note his ease around fellow pilots and old friends, such as those he met in Little Falls, Minnesota. Bruce Larson reports on these private and public appearances in "Lindbergh's Return to Minnesota in 1927," published in *Minnesota History* (Winter 1970). Other reminiscences—from Birmingham, Alabama, to Seattle, Washington—reflect the paradoxical nature of a private, rather shy young man's commitment to public enterprise.

Lindbergh's occasional aversion to the press and to crowds did not interrupt his goodwill flights, however. When his continental tour was over in November 1927, he took on another flight to Central and South America at the request of Dwight Morrow, ambassador to Mexico and his future father-in-law. Russell Owen captures the significance of the tour in "Lindbergh's Historic Central American Flight," published in *Current History* (1928). Lindbergh's hop from Washington, D.C., to Mexico City was nearly as symbolic as the New York to Paris flight, for it healed U.S. relations with Mexico and united the Hispanic peoples with their big brother to the north. The significance of his continuing flights to several Latin American nations is reflected nicely in Wesley P. Newton's "The Third Flight: Charles A. Lindbergh and Aviation Diplomacy in Latin America," *American Aviation Historical Society Journal* (1975). The tremendous crowds who came out to see "Lucky Lindy" were pleased with his gracious acceptance of their attention and his gentlemanly dealings with their leaders. They began to see the United States in a new light and eventually opened up the South to mail delivery and trade.

After Lindbergh had settled on a career in commercial aviation, he continued to fly in support of Transcontinental Air Transport and Pan American Airlines. The "Lindbergh Line" across the United States occupied him first, but he and Anne also made long mapping flights to the Orient via the polar cap and across the North and South Atlantic. These contributions to the growth of commercial flying are an important part of Henry L. Smith's *Airways: The History of Commercial Aviation in the United States* (1942). Smith chronicles TAT's change into the present-day TWA, as well as Pan Am's remarkable expansion into overseas markets during the 1930s. He also includes interesting material on Lindbergh's association with Igor Sikorsky, whose flying boats made initial overseas flights possible. Juan T. Trippe's brief pamphlet, *Charles A. Lindbergh and World Travel* (1977), adds details on Lindbergh's technical decisions and talent in aircraft design.

The best accounts of the Lindberghs' long flights in 1931 and 1933 are still in Anne M. Lindbergh's *North to the Orient* (1935) and *Listen! The Wind* (1938). She captures all the uncertainty and danger of their fog-bound voyages through uncharted territory in these two beautifully written books. The maps and notes by Charles add to their value as historical documents. Of course, these flights were also significant to aircraft design, because any plane able to fly such long distances with minimal mechanical support had to be state-of-the-art. This sometimes forgotten partner in the Lindberghs' successes is the subject of Richard S. Allen's "The Lockheed Sirius," included in the *American Aviation Historical Society Journal* (Winter 1965). Once again, Lindbergh combined love for adventure with careful planning and technical design to accomplish the remarkable.

The Kidnapping of Charles A. Lindbergh, Jr.

The volume of materials surrounding this infamous kidnapping case nearly rivals that of Lindbergh's transatlantic flight. Besides millions of words in newspapers across the nation, the event and its aftermath fostered dozens of books and articles. They fall essentially into two categories: accounts by contemporary observers or actors in the investigation and trial, or modern reconstructions and studies of the case's effect on the American justice system.

Every principle actor in this real-life tragedy has written about it, except Charles Lindbergh. Anne Lindbergh reports the shocking loss of her first-born son and the anguish of waiting to hear of his death in a volume of her diaries and letters: *Hour of Gold, Hour of Lead* (1973). Contemporary reporters John Brant and Edith Renaud recount the details of the crime in *True Story of the Lindbergh Kidnapping* (1932), and Laura Vitray constructs a provocative commentary on the events in *The Great Lindbergh Hullabaloo* (1932), suggesting that circumstances required an inside informant and more than one person to commit the crime. Sidney Whipple, who was the court reporter in the Bruno Richard Hauptmann trial, reconstructs the night of the kidnapping from court evidence in *The Lindbergh Crime* (1935).

The kidnapping trial, including police investigations that led to Hauptmann's arrest, has attracted far more commentary than the crime itself. Again Whipple used the court proceedings to relate main trial details in *The Trial of Bruno Richard Hauptmann* (1937). J. Vreeland Haring, a handwriting expert who testified that Hauptmann penned a ransom note and several succeeding notes demanding payment, wrote his version of the trial in *The Hand of Hauptmann* (1937). John F. (Jafsie) Condon, who worked with Lindbergh as an intermediary to obtain the release of Charles, Jr., reveals his part in the case in *Jafsie Tells All!* (1936). Each of these first-hand stories includes some interesting information about the kidnapping, but all are limited by circumstantial evidence and personal viewpoints.

Even modern commentators have found it difficult to avoid taking sides on the case, however. Andrew K. Dutch suggests that emotional reactions to the death of Lindbergh's baby disallowed a rational judgment of Hauptmann's guilt in *Hysteria: Lindbergh Kidnap Case* (1975). Anthony Scaduto takes this opinion even further, determining from the start that Hauptmann was innocent of the crime in *Scapegoat: The Lonesome Death of Bruno Richard Hauptmann* (1976). In a similarly slanted book, Theon Wright's *In Search of the Lindbergh Baby* (1981), the author attempts to show that mob elements commissioned the kidnapping. He goes on to suggest that the Lindbergh baby was left with a couple in the Midwest and that he has grown up to be Harold Olson. Most of his book hinges on inconclusive comparisons of closeup photographs and complaints about missing fingerprints from the Lindbergh case files, which might have proved Olson's case. Unfortunately, his thesis keeps him from acknowledging that many pieces of evidence led directly to Hauptmann.

Although it was possible that others were involved in the kidnapping, Louis M. Seidman finds no reason to doubt Hauptmann's guilt in his carefully argued legal article for the *Georgetown Law Journal* (October 1977): "The Trial and Execution of Bruno Richard Hauptmann." Another objective account, George Waller's *Kidnap: The Story of the Lindbergh Case* (1961), comes to the same conclusion. The case has now been officially reopened by the state of New Jersey, so the answers may be forthcoming. In the meantime, Waller's book and Seidman's article appear to be the best sources of information about the kidnap and trial.

World War II: Nonintervention and Service

Besides Lindbergh's *Wartime Journals* (1970) and *Of Flight and Life* (1948), as well as several of the full-length biographies cited above, a few pieces concentrate on his experiences before and during World War II. The best summary of his anti-intervention activities is in Wayne S. Cole's *America First: The Battle Against Intervention, 1940-1941* (1971) and, especially, *Charles A. Lindbergh and the Battle Against American Intervention in World War II* (1974). This latter book begins with Lindbergh's private conversations against intervention from 1936 on and moves the reader into his speeches and other activities from 1939-1941. Although Cole's work gives us an important and necessary look at Lindbergh's role, it is often repetitive in its commentary. Organization into overlapping chapters is the cause; thus, America First activities appear from several different viewpoints, and Lindbergh's views are hashed over in a separate chapter entitled "Is Lindbergh a Nazi?" Still, the information is worth working for.

More personal views of Lindbergh during this period come from the
Diaries and Letters: 1930-1939 of Sir Harold Nicolson or from Anne
Lindbergh's *The Flower and the Nettle* (1976) and *War Within and Without*
(1980). Nicolson views Lindbergh as a stubborn, rather naive fellow,
whose opinions hardened into dogma and prejudice. A similar tone
appears in Roger Butterfield's "Lindbergh: Stubborn Young Man of
Strange Ideas Becomes a Leader of Wartime Opposition," which appeared in *Life* magazine in 1941. Anne Lindbergh's diaries go a long way
to demonstrate Lindbergh's integrity and purity of motives, while
admitting that the issues themselves were very difficult to pin down in
the absence of certainty.

Even today, many people see Charles as a Nazi sympathizer before the
war, largely because so much news space was devoted to calling him
one. Three pamphlets in the Minnesota Historical Society's collection at
St. Paul show just how vitriolic the reaction against Lindbergh's
speeches became by 1941. Francis E. McMahon compiled a booklet for
the American Irish Defense Association called *Lindbergh and the Jews*
(1942). Numerous statements by famous Americans impugn Lindbergh's
remarks against Jewish influences on American policy and call for a
public apology. *American's Answer to Lindbergh* (1941), published by the
Minnesota Anti-Defamation Council, includes forty pages of clippings
against this same Des Moines, Iowa, speech on September 11, 1941.
Even more programmatic is L. M. Birkhead's *Is Lindbergh a Nazi?* (1941).
This pamphlet reviews Lindbergh's "fascist" sentiments by comparing
excerpts of his speeches to public statements by Hitler or leaders of
other pro-Nazi groups.

Although many members of America First and others opposed to the
war (including some prominent Jews) rushed to Lindbergh's defense,
only his actual service in defense of the nation could repair his damaged
reputation. Truman Smith's unpublished account of Lindbergh's intelligence activities from 1936 on helps to establish that service. His
163-page report on *Air Intelligence Activities* (1935-1939) at the Military
Attaché's office in Berlin demonstrates that every vital piece of information
on German airpower available to the U.S. State Department came from
Lindbergh's observations. He also points out that the award of the
German Cross, which had caused so much controversy, occurred at an
official state dinner held by the American ambassador. Charles was a
guest of the ambassador, thus having no recourse but to accept the German medal for his transatlantic flight. Once the war began, of course,
Lindbergh was an active member of the defense community. His actual
combat experience is chronicled in Charles MacDonald's "Lindbergh in
Battle," an article written for *Collier's* magazine (February 1946) and in
Lauren D. Lyman's "Operation Zero" for *Aero Digest* (May 1952). These
materials show how Lindbergh coped with a very difficult period in his

life—when his country rejected him for committing himself to its safety and to its ideals of free speech and citizenship.

Lindbergh and the Press

Lindbergh's relationship with the press is the subject of numerous articles in newspapers and journals. On one hand, he courted the press to advance aviation, recognizing their value in mobilizing the public to support progress in aircraft development, airfields, and commercial travel. On the other, he could never accept the public hunger for personal information, fanned by inaccurate press speculations. Neither could he condone the abusive, unethical practices of unscrupulous reporters and photographers, who intruded upon his home and family. This need-hate syndrome fascinated a number of commentators, who tried to discover reasons for his secretive behavior, disguises, and obvious delight in foiling news coverage of his activities.

The Lindberghs' point of view emerges from Anne Lindbergh's diaries, especially *Bring Me a Unicorn* (1972) and *Hour of Gold, Hour of Lead* (1973). She describes their trouble in going anywhere without public intrusion. Always an object of attention, always looked at, they began to adopt unusual methods to avoid scrutiny. Disguises, diversions, and false plans all became ways to gain their privacy. Other observers disagreed with their methods, however, believing that they simply called more attention to themselves with secrecy and outlandish getups. In "Privacy and the Lindberghs," an article for *Fortnightly Review* (1936), St. John Ervine suggests that the Lindberghs deserved some privacy, but anyone who seeks the public stage with his activities must expect to lose much of it. Similar themes appear in J. S. Gregory's "What's Wrong with Lindbergh," published in *Outlook* (December 1930) and in Silas Bent's "Lindbergh and the Press," also written for *Outlook* (April 1932). Sympathetic editorials in *Nation* (August 1930) and *New Republic* (June 1929) agreed that fame has a high cost to the person who attains it.

The serious consequences of fame struck the Lindberghs when Charles, Jr., was kidnapped in 1932, and the press reached its blackest hour in its handling of the crime and the ensuing trial. An editorial entitled "Child Murder As Entertainment," which appeared in *Catholic World* (March 1935), reported how the press delighted in presenting unsavory details to the public. Their unscrupulous efforts to photograph the Lindberghs in their grief and to stir up speculation over the criminal investigation led M. Marshall to call it the "Biggest Show on Earth" in his article for *Nation* (January 1935). When photographers attempted to break into the morgue for pictures of Charles, Jr.'s, remains and when others ran a car carrying Jon Lindbergh off the road for more pictures of the Lindberghs' second-born, Charles determined to live in England. Lauren D. Lyman's

Pulitzer Prize-winning news story, "Lindbergh Family Sails for England to Seek Safe, Secluded Residence," in the *New York Times* for December 23, 1935, pointed out their general travail and sadly noted the part played by an unruly press.

So predominant is this tragic irony of fame and privacy that all Lindbergh's biographers and commentators must deal with it. Two excellent resources for a study of its influences on Lindbergh's life as a whole are "The Price of Fame," a long article in the *New York Times Magazine* (May 8, 1977), and James A. Skardone's and Rosanne McVay's "Flight from Fame," published in *Coronet* (July 1957). Each pictures Lindbergh as essentially a private, even shy man, made famous by a hero-building press before he was equipped to deal with the consequences. Thereafter, he was compelled to live in the public arena, unable even to share casual conversation with people for fear of being misquoted or misrepresented. Finally, his position in the public eye led to the death of his first child, as well as his own alienation from close friends and much of American society during World War II. Such was the price of fame.

Lindbergh and Science

Because science was so much a part of Lindbergh's career, it is well to mark off a few sources for information on his scientific investigations. Besides his own articles and *The Culture of Organs*, coauthored with Alexis Carrel, several good articles discuss Lindbergh's contributions to archeology, biology, space programs, and medicine. Edward M. Weyer, Jr., reports on Lindbergh's use of the airplane to help discover Mayan ruins in "Exploring Cliff Dwellings with the Lindberghs," *World's Work* (December 1929). William Van Dusen's "Exploring the Maya with Lindbergh," written for the *Saturday Evening Post* (January 1930), adds some details from other flights. Lindbergh became interested in exploring the ruins while on his Central American tour in 1928.

Another avocation was biological research. F. C. Meier's "Collecting Microorganisms from the Arctic Atmosphere," in the January 1935 issue of *Scientific Monthly*, describes Lindbergh's invention of a "sky hook" and other collection devices, which allowed him to take samples of bacteria and plant spores from the atmosphere while in flight. Ranes C. Chakravorty adds to these details in his article on Charles's experiments in aerospace medicine and the centrifuging of whole blood: "Charles A. Lindbergh: Bio-engineer and Biologist" (*Scalpel and Tongs*, Summer 1977). Lindbergh's research with Carrel informs Arthur Train, Jr.'s, "More Will Live: Work of Carrel and Lindbergh," in the *Saturday Evening Post* (July 1938). This excellent article shows the significance of Charles's perfusion pump to medical surgery.

Lindbergh's involvement in the U.S. space program stemmed from encouragement of rocket research through Robert Goddard and the Ames Laboratory to improvements in space medicine at Brooks AFB, Texas. Milton Lehman sketches the former in "How Lindbergh Gave a Life to Rocketry," an excerpt from his book on Robert Goddard, which appeared in *Life* magazine in October 1963. And Douglas Rolfe points out some of Lindbergh's contributions to the space program in "From the *Spirit* to Space," an article for the Ryan Aeronautical Company *Reporter* (Summer 1967). Finally, Richard J. Bing summarizes most of these accomplishments in his editorial for the *Los Angeles Times* (September 25, 1974)—"The Public Knew Lindbergh as a Pilot, but He Explored Science, Too."

Lindbergh and Conservation

Always attracted to nature since his early days on the farm in Little Falls, Minnesota, Lindbergh became deeply involved in conservation during the last fifteen years of his life. Documentation of these interests is a bit sketchy, but still worthy of separate note here. His battle against the supersonic transport (SST) began once he recognized its ill effects on the environment. Two articles in the *New York Times* show how he helped stop the SST from operating in the United States: "Lindbergh Names Two Key SST Defects: Warns of Sonic Boom and Upper Air Pollution" (23 March 1971) and "Lindbergh Opposes Further SST Work" (6 February 1971). This decision was in line with his general turning away from technology if its dangers outweighed its advantages to mankind.

A few additional sources show his influence in saving species from extinction. For young readers, C. B. Squire reviews his saving of the whales off Peru and other conservation projects in a six-page section of *Heroes of Conservation* (1974). Rudolph Chelminski's "The Lindberghs Liberate Monkeys from Constraints" (*Smithsonian*, 1977); B. Goldwater's "Lone Eagle's Concern for the Bald Eagle" (*Saturday Review*, 1970); and John Nance's "Lindbergh Helps Philippines in Saving Monkey Eagle" (*Philadelphia Enquirer*, July 1971) reveal how active Lindbergh was in the waning years of his life. An editorial in the April 9, 1972 issue of the *New York Times*, called "Going Back Time," and John Nance's *The Gentle Tasaday* (1975) tell the story of Lindbergh's last great cause—saving the Stone-Age Tasadays from the encroachments of civilization.

Together, these bibliographical records reflect a complex man in a complex age. To read the varied materials on the life of Charles A. Lindbergh is to know much of American society in the twentieth century.

5

A SELECTIVE BIBLIOGRAPHY

The following checklist is, by necessity, limited in scope. But my choosing to omit or include particular items isn't entirely idiosyncratic. Most newspaper pieces are either less substantial than or nearly identical to similar articles in magazines or journals, which are much easier to access. Also, editorial statements in weekly magazines simply don't add anything to information from journals and books. Yet, I've included some weeklies or newspapers when their contents reflect the range of Lindbergh's newsworthiness.

A few words about arrangement and method will also be helpful. For works by Lindbergh, the listing is chronological—following common practice and the most likely needs of researchers. All secondary sources are alphabetized within categories by title or author's last name. I have penned short parenthetical comments to clarify the content of some entries; they appear immediately after bibliographical information. I've tried to view as many of these sources as possible, but I have relied on standard indexes for a number of them. Thus, some authors appear with initials rather than full first names, and a few references don't list page numbers throughout an article with intermittent pagination.

Finally, I gratefully acknowledge the contributions of previous researchers, without whose work this compilation would have been far more arduous. Arthur G. Renstrom's selective bibliography for the Library of Congress *Information Bulletin* (13 and 20 May, 1977) and Dominick A. Pisano's listing in *Charles A. Lindbergh: An American Life*, pp. 105-119 (see below) were most helpful.

LINDBERGH'S WRITINGS

Notice by Cadet Charles A. Lindbergh of Parachute Jump made at Kelly Field, Texas, 6 March 1925. *Air Service News Letter* 6 (12 April 1925):6-7.
"Going Over the Side Three Times with a Parachute." *U.S. Air Services* 12 (February 1927):42-43.
"Lindbergh's Own Story of Epochal Flight." *New York Times*, 23 May 1927, 1:5-8 and 2:1-4. [First installment of a series continued May 24, 28, 29, 31 and

June 1, 2, 3, 5, 9, 10, 11. Ghost written. Lindbergh called it "a highly in-accurate account." Appears consolidated in *Current History*, 26 (July 1927): 513-522.]

"And Then I Jumped." *Saturday Evening Post* 200 (23 July 1927):6-7.

"Report of Northbound Mail Flight, 3 November 1926, by Charles A. Lindbergh, Pilot, Contract Air Mail, No. 2." *Review of Reviews* 76 (August 1927): 202-204.

We: The Famous Flier's Own Story of His Life and Transatlantic Flight. Foreword by Myron T. Herrick. New York: G. P. Putnam's Sons, 1927. (Also published New York: Grosset and Dunlap, 1927. Includes "A Little of What the World Thought of Lindbergh," by Fitzhugh Green, pp. 233-318.)

"The Making of an Air Mail Pilot: The Unforgettable Thrills of the First Solo Flight." *World's Work*, 54 (September 1927):472-481.

"To Bogota and Back by Air." *National Geographic Magazine*, 53 (May 1928): 529-601. (Account of the Latin American goodwill tour.)

Address on the Need for the Study and Teaching of Elementary Aeronautics in the American School System. *Proceedings of the 66th Annual Meeting at Minneapolis, Minnesota, July 1-6, 1928*, vol. 66. Minneapolis: n.p., 1928, pp. 808-809.

"Air Transport." *Saturday Evening Post*, 202 (1 February 1930):7, 50.

"Future of the Glider." *New York Times*, 23 March 1930, section 10, p. 1.

"Apparatus to Circulate Liquid Under Constant Pressure In a Closed System." *Science*, 73 (1931):566.

"Method for Washing Corpuscles in Suspension." *Science*, 75 (15 April 1932): 415-416.

Foreword to "Flying around the North Atlantic," by Anne M. Lindbergh. *National Geographic Magazine*, 66 (September 1934):259-337. (A survey trip of 29,000 miles: July 9-December 9, 1933.)

Field Notes and Material to "Collecting Microorganisms from the Arctic Atmosphere," by F. C. Meier. *Scientific Monthly*, 40 (January 1935):5-20.

Maps to *North to the Orient*, by Anne M. Lindbergh. New York: Harcourt, Brace and Company, 1935.

With Alexis Carrel, "The Culture of Whole Organs." *Science*, 81 (21 June 1935): 621-623.

"An Apparatus for the Culture of Whole Organs." *The Journal of Experimental Medicine* 62 (1 September 1935):409-431.

"Aviation and War." *Vital Speeches of the Day* 2 (1 August 1936):696. (Delivered at a luncheon given in his honor by the German Air Ministry in Berlin, 23 July 1936.)

With Alexis Carrel, *The Culture of Organs*. New York: P. B. Hoeber, 1938.

Foreword and Map Drawings to *Listen! The Wind*, by Anne M. Lindbergh. New York: Harcourt, Brace and Company, 1938.

Statement on Air Corps Expansion Program. In U.S. House Committee on Appropriations Hearings . . . on the Supplemental Military Appropriation Bill for 1940. Washington: U.S. Government Printing Office, 1939, pp. 288-290.

"A Culture Flask for the Circulation of a Large Quantity of Fluid Medium." *The Journal of Experimental Medicine* 70 (1 September 1939):231-238.

"Appeal for Isolation." *Vital Speeches of the Day* 5 (1 October 1939):751-752. (Text of radio address from Washington, D.C., 15 September 1939.)

"Aviation, Geography, and Race." *Reader's Digest* 35 (November 1939):64-67.

"What Our Decision Should Be." *Vital Speeches of the Day* 6 (1 November 1939): 57-59.

"What Substitute for War?" *Atlantic Monthly* 165 (March 1940):304-308.

"Our National Safety." *Vital Speeches of the Day* 6 (1 June 1940):484-485. (Text of radio address, 19 May 1940.)

"Our Drift Toward War." *Vital Speeches of the Day* 6 (1 July 1940):549-551. (Text of radio address, 15 June 1940.)

"Appeal for Peace." *Vital Speeches of the Day* 6 (15 August 1940):644-646. (Delivered at a Keep-America-Out-Of-War rally, Chicago, 4 August 1940.)

"Strength and Peace." *Vital Speeches of the Day* 7 (1 November 1940):42-43. (Text of radio address from Washington, D.C., 13 October 1940.)

"Plea for American Independence." *Scribner's Commentator* 9 (December 1940):69-73. (Text of radio address, 14 October 1939.)

The Radio Addresses of Charles A. Lindbergh. New York: *Scribner's Commentator,* 1940. (Contents: "American and European Wars," "Neutrality and War," "The Air Defense of America," "Our Drift toward War," "Our Relationship with Europe.")

"Impregnable America." *Scribner's Commentator* 9 (January 1941):3-6. (Part of an address at Yale University, 30 October 1940.)

"Our Air Defense." *Vital Speeches of the Day* 7 (1 February 1941):241-242. (Testimony before the House Foreign Affairs Committee, 23 January 1941.)

"We Are Not Prepared for War." *Vital Speeches of the Day* 7 (15 February 1941): 266-267. (Testimony before the Senate Foreign Relations Committee, 6 February 1941.)

"A Letter to Americans." *Collier's* 107 (29 March 1941):75-77.

"We Cannot Win This War for England." *Vital Speeches of the Day* 7 (1 May 1941): 424-426. (Speech at the America First Committee meeting in New York's Manhattan Center, 23 April 1941.)

"Election Promises Should Be Kept." *Vital Speeches of the Day* 7 (1 June 1941): 482-483. (Delivered at Madison Square Garden, 23 May 1941.)

"Lindbergh for the Record: Views on the Great Controversial Issues of the Day." *Scribner's Commentator* 10 (August 1941):7-13. (Lindbergh's views on Germany, British Empire, foreign policy, intervention, defense, democracy, America, unity, and leadership.)

"Who Are the War Agitators?" *Des Moines Register,* 12 September 1941, 6:1, and *Chicago Tribune,* 12 September 1941, 1:6 and 10:6-8. (Delivered at the Des Moines Coliseum, 11 September 1941, this infamous speech named the British, the Jews, and the Roosevelt administration as chief agitators for war.)

"My Last Address." *Time* 38 (13 October 1941):15. (Excerpts from an address at Fort Wayne, Indiana.)

"Time Lies with Us." *Scribner's Commentator* 11 (November 1941):88-93. (Speech delivered at the Hollywood Bowl in Los Angeles, California.)

Of Flight and Life. New York: Charles Scribner's Sons, 1948.

"A Lesson from the Wright Brothers." *Aviation Week* 51 (26 December 1949):42. [Lindbergh's acceptance speech on receiving the 1949 Wright Brothers Memorial Trophy at the Aero Club in Washington, D.C., 17 December 1949. Also published with the title "Man Cannot Thrive Independently in the Hot-House Atmosphere We Are Creating" in *U.S. Air Services* 35 (January 1950):11, 13, and with the title "Human Qualities Must Keep Pace with Science" in *National Aeronautics and Flight Plan* 29 (January 1950):6.]

Preface to *The Voyage to Lourdes*, by Alexis Carrel. Translated from the French by Virgilia Peterson. New York: Harper, 1950.

The Spirit of St. Louis. New York: Charles Scribner's Sons, 1953. (Won the Pulitzer Prize for biography in May 1954.)

"The Fourth Dimension of Survival." *Saturday Review* 37 (27 February 1954): 11-12. [Published also with title "I Have Stated a Problem; You Have the Right to Ask Me for a Solution" in *U.S. Air Services* 39 (March 1954):17-19; as "The Future Character of Man" in *Vital Speeches of the Day* 20 (1 March 1954):293-295; as "Honors Night Dinner Address" in *Aeronautical Engineering Review* 13 (March 1954):48-51, 87; and abridged as "But How About Man?" in *Reader's Digest* 64 (May 1954):1-2. An address delivered at the Honors Night Dinner of the Institute of Aeronautical Sciences, Hotel Astor, New York, 25 January 1954. Lindbergh received the Daniel Guggenheim Medal for pioneering in flight and aerial navigation.]

"Our Best Chance to Survive." *Saturday Evening Post* 227 (17 July 1954):25.

"Thoughts of a Combat Pilot." *Saturday Evening Post* 227 (2 October 1954):20-21, 78, 80. [Abridged as "The Church in the Gunsight" in *Reader's Digest* 65 (December 1954):11-14.]

Introduction to *Winning the War with Ships*, by Emory Scott Land. New York: Robert M. McBride, 1958.

Preface to *This High Man: The Life of Robert H. Goddard*, by Milton Lehman. New York: Farrar, Straus and Giroux, 1963.

"Is Civilization Progress?" *Reader's Digest* 25 (July 1964):67-74.

Foreword to *Challenge to the Poles: Highlights of Arctic and Antarctic Aviation*, by John Grierson. Hamden, Connecticut: Archon Books, 1964.

With V. P. Perry, Theodore I. Malinin, and G. H. Mouer. "An Apparatus for the Pulsating Perfusion of Whole Organs." *Cryobiology* 3 (1966):252-260.

"Wisdom of Wildness." *Life* 63 (22 December 1967):8-10. [Published also in *Reader's Digest* (April 19678):83-87.]

"A Letter from Lindbergh." *Life* 67 (4 July 1969): 60A-61. (Special issue of *Life* entitled "Off to the Moon," in which Lindbergh states: "I have turned my attention from technological progress to life, from the civilized to the wild.")

Foreword to *Vanguard: A History*, by Constance M. Green and Milton Lomask. Washington, D.C.: Smithsonian Institution Press, 1971. (Foreword is dated 11 August 1969; tells of Lindbergh's contacts with the American satellite program.)

Introduction to *Maui: The Last Hawaiian Place*. San Francisco and New York: Friends of the Earth, 1970.

The Wartime Journals of Charles A. Lindbergh. New York: Harcourt Brace Jovanovich, 1970. [Excerpted in *American Scholar* 39 (August 1970):577-613, and in *American Heritage* 21 (October 1970):32-37, 114-115.]

"The Way of Wildness." *Reader's Digest* 99 (November 1971):90-93.

Foreword to *Alexis Carrel: Visionary Surgeon*, by W. Stirling Edwards and Peter D. Edwards. Springfield, Ill.: Thomas, 1971.

"Feel the Earth." *Reader's Digest* 101 (July 1972):62-65.

"For Me, Aviation Has Value Only to the Extent that It Contributes to the Quality of the Human Life It Serves." *New York Times*, 27 July 1972, 31:2-4. (Stating that the supersonic transport shouldn't be allowed to fly over U.S. territory if its effect on the environment is unsatisfactory.)

"Lessons from the Primitive." *Reader's Digest* 101 (November 1972):147-151.

Boyhood on the Upper Mississippi: A Reminiscent Letter. St. Paul: Minnesota Historical Society, 1972.

Foreword to *Lindbergh of Minnesota: A Political Biography*, by Bruce L. Larson. New York: Harcourt Brace Jovanovich, 1973.

"Some Remarks at the Dedication of Lindbergh State Park Interpretive Center." *Minnesota History* 43 (Fall 1973):275-276.

Foreword to *Carrying the Fire: An Astronaut's Journey*, by Michael Collins. New York: Farrar, Straus and Giroux, 1974.

Foreword to *The Gentle Tasaday: A Stone-Age People in the Philippine Rain Forest*, by John Nance. New York: Harcourt Brace Jovanovich, 1975. (Lindbergh finished this foreword in Hawaii five months before he died.)

Banana River. New York: Harcourt Brace Jovanovich, 1976. (A selection from unpublished autobiographical notes, compiled by Judith Schiff and William Jovanovich.)

An Autobiography of Values. New York: Harcourt Brace Jovanovich, 1978. (Edited by Judith Schiff and William Jovanovich.)

"Lindbergh Letter to a Congressman Reflects Philosophical Approach to Science Policy." *Science* 204 (29 June 1979):1392-1393.

BIOGRAPHICAL REFERENCES

Books and Pamphlets

America's Answer to Lindbergh. St. Paul: Minnesota Anti-Defamation Council, 1941. (Pamphlet: about forty pages of clippings from across the country condemning Lindbergh's "British, Jews, and Roosevelt Administration" speech at Des Moines, Iowa, on 11 September 1941.)

Beamish, Richard J. *The Story of Lindbergh: The Lone Eagle*. Philadelphia: International Press, 1927. (Juvenile. Also published as *The Boy's Story of Lindbergh: the Lone Eagle*. Philadelphia: John C. Winston, 1928.)

Birkhead, L. M. *Is Lindbergh a Nazi?* Chicago: Friends of Democracy, 1941. (Pamphlet: twenty-seven pages, reviewing "fascist" sentiments of Charles Lindbergh. In the collection of the Minnesota Historical Society at St. Paul, Minnesota.)

Brant, John, and Edith Renaud. *True Story of the Lindbergh Kidnapping*. New York: Kroy Wen Publishers, 1932.

Burden, James H. *An Interpretation of Colonel Lindbergh's Achievements*. Sacramento, n.p., 1928.

Cole, Wayne S. *America First: The Battle Against Intervention, 1940-1941*. Reprint. New York: Octagon Books, 1971. (Extensive material on Lindbergh's involvement with the America First Committee.)

———. *Charles A. Lindbergh and the Battle against American Intervention in World War II*. New York: Harcourt Brace Jovanovich, 1974.

Collins, David R. *Charles Lindbergh: Hero Pilot*. Illustrated by Victor Mays. Champaign, Illinois: Garrard, 1978. (Juvenile.)

Condon, John F. *Jafsie Tells All! Revealing the Inside Story of the Lindbergh-Hauptmann Case*. New York: Jonathan Lee, 1936.

Coolidge, Calvin. *Address at the Awarding . . . of the Hubbard Medal*. Washington, D.C.: U.S. Government Printing Office, 1927. (Pamphlet.)

_____. *Address Bestowing on Charles A. Lindbergh the Distinguished Flying Cross*. Washington, D.C.: U.S. Government Printing Office, 1927. (Pamphlet)

Crouch, Tom D., ed. *Charles A. Lindbergh: An American Life*. Washington, D.C.: National Air and Space Museum, 1977. (Contents: "Introduction" pp. xiii-xv; John Grierson, "Charles A. Lindbergh," pp. 3-14; Paul R. Ignatius, "Every Flight for a Purpose," pp. 15-22; Richard P. Hallion, "Charles A. Lindbergh and Aviation Technology," pp. 39-48; Wayne S. Cole, "Charles A. Lindbergh and the Battle against Intervention," pp. 49-56; Judith Schiff, "Values of Flight and Life: The Postwar Activities," pp. 71-81; Donald A. Hall, "Technical Preparation of the Airplane 'Spirit of St. Louis,' " pp. 83-93; Dominick A. Pisano, "A Selected Bibliography," pp. 105-119; photos: pp. 23-37, 57-69, and 94-104.)

Dalgliesh, Alice. *Ride On the Wind*. New York: Charles Scribner's Sons, 1956. (Juvenile.)

Davis, Kenneth S. *Flight to Glory: The Story of Charles A. Lindbergh and the Spirit of St. Louis*. Illustrated by John N. Barron. Garden City, N.Y.: Garden City Books, 1960. (Juvenile.)

_____. *The Hero: Charles A. Lindbergh and the American Dream*. Garden City, N.Y.: Doubleday and Co., 1959. (Includes long bibliographical essay, pp. 434-515.)

DeLeeuw, Adele L. *Lindbergh: Lone Eagle*. Philadelphia: The Westminister Press, 1969. (Juvenile.)

Dutch, Andrew K. *Hysteria: Lindbergh Kidnap Case*. Philadelphia: Dorrance, 1975.

Fago, John N. *Charles Lindbergh*. Pendulum Illustrated Biography Series. West Haven, Connecticut: Pendulum Press, 1979. (Juvenile.)

Fife, George B. *Lindbergh the Lone Eagle: His Life and Achievements*. New York: World Syndicate, 1927. (1933 edition adds accounts of Lindbergh's U.S. and Latin American tours.)

Fisk, Nicholas. *Lindbergh the Lone Flier*. Illustrated by Raymond Briggs. London: Hamish Hamilton, Ltd., 1968. (Juvenile. Unpaginated, illustrated account of the transatlantic flight.)

Foster, John T. *The Flight of the Lone Eagle*. New York: Franklin Watts, 1974. (Juvenile.)

Gage, Gerald R., and James Lindbergh. *"Plucky" Lindbergh*. Los Angeles: Gem, 1927. (Brief biography and miscellany in a vernacular style.)

Gill, Brendan. *Lindbergh Alone*. New York: Harcourt Brace Jovanovich, 1977.

Grierson, John. *I Remember Lindbergh*. New York: Harcourt Brace Jovanovich, 1977. (Flier John Grierson's personal recollections of Lindbergh, with an introduction by Anne M. Lindbergh.)

Gross, Ruth B. *Dangerous Adventure! Lindbergh's Famous Flight*. Illustrated by Susanne Suba. New York: Scholastic Book Services, 1977. (Juvenile.)

Haring, J. Vreeland. *The Hand of Hauptmann*. Plainfield, N.J.: Hamer, 1937. (The Handwriting Expert Tells the Story of the Lindbergh Case.)

Keyhoe, Donald E. *Flying with Lindbergh*. New York: G. P. Putnam's Sons, 1928. (On the forty-eight-state flying tour in 1928.)

Kurland, Gerald. *Lindbergh Flies the Atlantic*. Events of Our Times, no. 19. Charlotteville, N.Y.: Sam Har Press, 1975. (Juvenile.)

Leipold, L. Edmond. *Charles A. Lindbergh, Aviation Pioneer*. Men of Achievement Series. Minneapolis: T. S. Denison and Co., 1972.

Lindbergh, Anne M. *Bring Me a Unicorn: Diaries and Letters of Anne Morrow Lindbergh, 1922-1928*. New York: Harcourt Brace Jovanovich, 1972.

———. *The Flower and the Nettle: Diaries and Letters of Anne Morrow Lindbergh, 1936-1939*. New York: Harcourt Brace Jovanovich, 1976.

———. *Hour of Gold, Hour of Lead: Diaries and Letters of Anne Morrow Lindbergh, 1929-1932*. New York: Harcourt Brace Jovanovich, 1973.

———. *Listen! The Wind*. New York: Harcourt Brace, 1938.

———. *Locked Rooms and Open Doors: Diaries and Letters of Anne Morrow Lindbergh, 1933-1935*. New York: Harcourt Brace Jovanovich, 1974.

———. *North to the Orient*. New York: Harcourt Brace, 1935.

———. *War Within and Without: Diaries and Letters of Anne Morrow Lindbergh, 1939-1944*. New York: Harcourt Brace Jovanovich, 1980.

———. *The Wave of the Future: A Confession of Faith*. New York: Harcourt Brace, 1940.

The Lone Eagle: Lindbergh. Chicago: The Blakely Printing Company, 1929. (Juvenile "picture book.")

McMahon, Francis E. *Lindbergh and the Jews*. Boston: American Irish Defense Association, 1942. (Pamphlet.)

Miller, Francis T. *Lindbergh: His Story in Pictures*. New York: G. P. Putnam's Sons, 1929.

Mosley, Leonard. *Lindbergh: A Biography*. Garden City, N.Y.: Doubleday, 1976.

Prosser, Charles A. *Information Book on Taking a Look at Yourself*. Bloomington, Illinois: McKnight and McKnight, 1937. (Juvenile advice book, using Lindbergh as a model.)

Reeves, Earl. *Lindbergh Flies On!* New York: Robert M. McBride and Co., 1929.

Richards, Kenneth G. *Charles Lindbergh*. People of Destiny Series. Chicago: Children's Press, 1968 (Illustrated juvenile biography.)

Ross, Walter S. *The Last Hero: Charles A. Lindbergh*. New York: Harper and Row, 1976.

Scaduto, Anthony. *Scapegoat: The Lonesome Death of Bruno Richard Hauptmann*. New York: G. P. Putnam's Sons, 1976.

Shoenfeld, Dudley D. *The Crime and the Criminal: A Psychiatric Study of the Lindbergh Case*. New York: Covici-Friede, 1936.

Smith, Truman. Air Intelligence Activities, Office of the Military Attaché American Embassy, Berlin, Germany, August 1935-April 1939, with Special Reference to the Services of Colonel Charles A. Lindbergh, Air Corps (Res.) (Unpublished memoir, 1954-1956, in the manuscript collection of the Yale University Library, New Haven, Connecticut.)

Snell, Dewitt S. *The Lindberghs—an Appreciation*. Schenectady, N.Y.: n.p., 1941. (Pamphlet. Reports Lindbergh's keeping a self-improvement chart.)

Stroud, John. *Spirit of St. Louis: Charles Lindbergh's Solo Transatlantic Flight*. London: Orbis Publishing, 1978.

Trippe, Juan T. *Charles A. Lindbergh and World Travel*. Fourteenth Wings Club

"Sight" Lecture. Presented at the Wings Club on 20 May 1977, in New York City. (Privately printed pamphlet in Library of Congress collection.)

U.S. Department of State. *The Flight of Captain Charles A. Lindbergh from New York to Paris, May 20-21, 1927, as Compiled from the Official Records of the Department of State*. Washington, D.C.: U.S. Government Printing Office, 1927.

Van Dusen, Earl C. *Lindbergh the Flier of Little Falls*. St. Cloud, Minnesota: n.p., 1928. (A dedication booklet from the High School Classes of 1928 and 1929.)

Van Every, Dale, and Morris DeHaven Tracy. *Charles Lindbergh, His Life*. New York: D. Appleton and Co., 1927.

Van Kampen, Isaac. *Lindbergh: A Saga of Youth*. Boston: Stratford Company, 1928.

Vitray, Laura. *The Great Lindbergh Hullabaloo: An Unorthodox Account*. New York: William Faro, 1932. (An account of the Lindbergh kidnapping.)

Waller, George. *Kidnap. The Story of the Lindbergh Case*. New York: Dial Press, 1961.

Wendel, Paul H. *The Lindbergh-Hauptmann Aftermath*. Brooklyn, N.Y.: Loft Publishing Co., 1940.

West, James E. *The Lone Scout of the Sky: The Story of Charles A. Lindbergh*. Philadelphia: John C. Winston, 1928. (An account for the Boy Scouts of America.)

Whipple, Sidney B. *The Lindbergh Crime*. New York: Blue Ribbon Books, 1935.

_____. *The Trial of Bruno Richard Hauptmann*. Garden City, N.Y.: Doubleday, 1937. (Court proceedings of the kidnapping trial resulting from the kidnap of Lindbergh's son, Charles Augustus, on 1 March 1932.)

Wise, William. *Charles A. Lindbergh: Aviation Pioneer*. An American Hero Biography. New York: G. P. Putnam's Sons, 1970.

Wray, Dorothy M., comp. Lindbergh Scrapbook. Campbell, Minnesota: n.p., 1927. (unpublished folio scrapbook of mounted newspaper clippings, in the Minnesota Historical Society collection at St. Paul, Minnesota.)

Wright, Theon. *In Search of the Lindbergh Baby*. New York: Tower Publications, 1981.

Sections, Chapters, or Articles in Books

Allen, Frederick L. "Lindbergh Case." In *Thirties*, edited by Don Congdon. New York: Simon and Schuster, 1962, pp. 206-210.

_____. *Only Yesterday*. New York: Harper and Brothers, 1931. (Contains a chapter on Lindbergh's transatlantic flight.)

The American Heritage History of Flight. New York: American Heritage, 1962. (Includes comments on Lindbergh's major exploratory flights.)

Ault, Phillip. *By the Seat of Their Pants*. New York: Dodd Mead, 1978, pp. 94-97 and 139-153.

Brennan, Dennis. *Adventures in Courage*. New York: Reilly and Lee, 1968, pp. 105-133.

Bruno, Harry A. *Wings Over America: The Story of American Aviation*. New York: Robert M. McBride, 1942. (Chapter 11: "Young Lindbergh.")

Canning, John, ed. *100 Great Modern Lives*. New York: Hawthorn, 1965, pp. 600-605.

Chant, Christopher. *Aviation, an Illustrated History*. New York: Crescent Books, 1980. (Comments on several of Lindbergh's flights.)

Churchill, Allen. *Remember When*. New York: Golden Press, 1967. (Juvenile. Includes "The Lone Eagle": pp. 214-219.)

Clark, Leonard. *When They Were Children*. New York: Roy, 1964, pp. 137-144. (Juvenile.)

Croix, Robert de la. *They Flew the Atlantic*. Translated from the French by Edward Fitzgerald. New York: W. W. Norton, 1959. (Chapter 5 is "Charles A. Lindbergh," pp. 82-99.)

Davis, Kenneth S. "The Flight." In *Early Air Pioneers: 1862-1935*, edited by James F. Sunderman. New York: Watts, 1961, pp. 210-218.

Delear, Frank J. *Igor Sikorsky: His Three Careers in Aviation*. New York: Dodd Mead, 1976. (Parts of this book reflect Lindbergh's association with Sikorsky.)

Drennan, Marguerite. *Thoroughbred Hearts*. New York: Comet, 1957, pp. 165-171.

Dwiggins, Don. *The Barnstormers: Flying Daredevils of the Roaring Twenties*. New York: Grosset and Dunlap, 1968, pp. 63-73.

Eubank, Nancy. *The Lindberghs: Three Generations*. St. Paul: Minnesota Historical Society, 1975. (Short pamphlet with sections on Charles Lindbergh at pp. 1-2 and 9-13.)

Faber, Harold, and Doris Faber. *American Heroes of the 20th Century*. New York: Random House, 1967, pp. 13-19. (Juvenile.)

Fitzhugh, Harriet L., and P. K. Fitzhugh. *Concise Biographical Dictionary of Famous Men and Women*. Rev. and enl. New York: Grosset and Dunlap, 1949, pp. 410-411.

Fitzpatrick, James K. *Builders of the American Dream*. New Rochelle, N.Y.: Arlington House, 1977, pp. 200-225.

Forsee, Aylesa. *My Love and I Together*. New York: Macrae, 1961, pp. 75-108. (Juvenile account of the Lindberghs' relationship as a model of sharing and mutual support.)

Fraser, Chelsea. *Famous American Flyers*. New York: Thomas Y. Crowell, 1941, pp. 151-179.

_____. *Heroes of the Air*. Rev. ed. New York: Thomas Y. Crowell, 1937. (Chapters 14, 16, 17, and 19 recount four of Lindbergh's exploratory flights.)

Goldstrom, John. *A Narrative History of Aviation*. New York: Macmillan, 1930, p. 223-250.

Guggenheim, Harry F. *The Seven Skies*. New York: G. P. Putnam's Sons, 1930. ("The Significance of the Lindbergh Flight," pp. 73-91.)

Hagedorn, Hermann. *Eleven Who Dared*. New York: Four Winds, 1966, pp. 129-143. (Juvenile.)

Haines, Lynn, and Dora B. Haines. *The Lindberghs*. New York: The Vanguard Press, 1931. (Concentrates chiefly on Lindbergh's father, Charles August Lindbergh, showing several character traits father and son had in common.)

Hallion, Richard P., Jr. *Legacy of Flight: The Guggenheim Contribution to American Aviation*. Seattle: University of Washington Press, 1977. (Parts of this book review Lindbergh's association with the Daniel Guggenhein Fund for the Promotion of Aeronautics.)

Hayman, Le Roy. *Aces, Heroes and Daredevils of the Air.* New York: Messner, 1981, pp. 99-110. (Juvenile.)

Hazeltine, Alice I., comp. *We Grew Up in America.* New York: Abingdon, 1954, pp. 174-184.

Heinmuller, John P. V. *Man's Fight to Fly.* New York: Funk and Wagnall, 1944, pp. 68-85.

Hoare, Robert J. *Wings Over the Atlantic.* London: Phoenix House, Ltd., 1956, pp. 45-56.

Hoyer, Eva H. *Sixteen Exceptional Americans.* New York: Vantage, 1959, pp. 341-360.

Hoyt, Edwin P. *Heroes of the Skies.* Garden City, N.Y.: Doubleday, 1963, pp. 85-97 and 118-119.

Hynd, A. "Everybody Wanted in the Act." In *Treasury of True.* New York: Barnes and Noble, 1956, pp. 17-45.

Jablonski, Edward. *Atlantic Fever.* New York: Macmillan, 1972, pp. 97-128.

James, E. L. "Lucky Lindy Takes a Trip." In *These Were the Years,* edited by Frank Brookhouser. Garden City, N.Y.: Doubleday, 1959, pp. 196-200.

Kaltenborn, Hans von. *It Seems Like Yesterday.* New York: G. P. Putnam's Sons, 1956, pp. 67-72.

Lardner, John. "The Lindbergh Legends." In *The Aspirin Age: 1919-1941,* edited by Isabel Leighton. New York: Simon and Schuster, 1949, pp. 190-213.

Lardner, Rex. *Ten Heroes of the Twenties.* New York: G. P. Putnam's Sons, 1966, pp. 91-115.

Lomask, Milton. *Seed Money: The Guggenheim Story.* New York: Farrar, Straus and Giroux, 1964. (Includes a recounting of Lindbergh's association with The Daniel Guggenheim Fund for the Promotion of Aeronautics.)

MacMillan, Norman. *Great Flights and Air Adventures.* New York: St. Martin's, 1965, pp. 165-179.

Mason, Herbert M., Jr. *Bold Men, Far Horizons.* Philadelphia: J. B. Lippincott, 1966.

Mears, Louise W. *They Come and Go.* New York: Christopher, 1955, pp. 106-112.

Mordenn, Ethan. *That Jazz! An Idiosyncratic Social History of the American Twenties.* New York: G. P. Putnam's Sons, 1978, pp. 236-278.

Morgan, David. *True Adventures of Railroaders.* New York: Little, Brown, 1954, pp. 96-111. (Juvenile.)

Nevin, David. *The Epic of Flight.* In *The Pathfinders,* a Time-Life Series, vol. 2. Alexandria, Va.: Time-Life Books, 1980.

Nicolson, Sir Harold. *Diaries and Letters: 1930-1939.* Edited by Nigel Nicolson. New York: Atheneum, 1966. (Many observations on the Lindberghs from the author's visits at their home and from the Lindberghs' renting of his cottage, Long Barn, in England between 1936 and 1938.)

————. *Dwight Morrow.* New York: Harcourt Brace, 1935. (This biography of Anne Morrow Lindbergh's father includes information about Charles Lindbergh.)

Niebuhr, Reinhold. *The Self and the Dramas of History.* New York: Charles Scribner's Sons, 1955, pp. 26-29. (Discusses Lindbergh's account of a dialogue with his "ghost" in *The Spirit of St. Louis.*)

O'Brien, Patrick J. *The Lindberghs: The Story of a Distinguished Family.* Philadelphia: International Press, 1935. (Contains interesting information on Charles and Anne Lindbergh.)

Paton, Graham, ed. *Great Men and Women of Modern Times*. New York: Purnell, 1968, pp. 62-63. (Juvenile.)

Phelps, George A. *Holidays and Philosophical Biographies*. New York: House-Warven, 1951, pp. 41-48.

Powell, Lucile R. *10 All-American Boys*. Philadelphia: Dorrance, 1971, pp. 27-34. (Juvenile.)

Pudney, John. *Six Great Aviators*. London: Hamish Hamilton, 1955, pp. 123-156. (Juvenile.)

Smith, Henry L. *Airways: The History of Commercial Aviation in the United States*. New York: Alfred Knopf, 1942. (Several references to Lindbergh's association with Igor Sikorsky, Pan American, and Transcontinental Air Transport during 1929-1940.)

Squire, C. B. *Heroes of Conservation*. Place Unknown: Fleet Press, 1974, pp. 72-79. (Juvenile.)

Stevenson, Elizabeth. *Babbits and Bohemians: The American 1920s*. New York: Macmillan, 1967.

Stewart, Oliver. *First Flights*. New York: Pitman Publishing, 1958, pp. 132-136.

Stone, Irving, and Richard Kennedy, eds. *We Speak for Ourselves*. Garden City, N.Y.: Doubleday, 1950, pp. 186-192.

Sufrin, Mark. *The Brave Men: Twelve Portraits of Courage*. Illustrated by Richard Smith. New York: Platt and Munk, 1967, pp. 53-79.

Sullivan, George. *They Flew Alone*. New York: Frederick Warner, 1969, pp. 74-83.

Tanner, Louise S. *Here Today. . . .* New York: Thomas Y. Crowell, 1959, pp. 35-49.

Taylor, John W. Ranson. *Great Moments in Flying*. New York: Roy, 1956, pp. 67-77.

Teale, Edwin W. *The Book of Gliders*. New York: E. P. Dutton, 1930. (Chapter 5, "Noted Glider Pilots," describes Lindbergh's gliding activities and his association with William Hawley Bowlus.)

Thomas, Lowell. *Famous First Flights that Changed History*. Garden City, N.Y.: Doubleday, 1968, pp. 145-165.

Van Der Linde, H. J. "How We Built Slim's 60-Day Wonder." As told to Eliot Tozer. In *Anthology of True*. New York: Nelson, 1962, pp. 210-216.

Walhauser, Henry T. *Pioneers of Flight*. Illustrated by Jack Woodson. Maplewood, N.J.: Hammond, 1969. (Juvenile.)

Walker, S. "Judging of Hauptmann." In *Thirties*, edited by Don Congdon. New York: Simon and Schuster, 1962, pp. 210-216.

Ward, John William. *Red, White, and Blue: Men, Books, and Ideas in American Culture*. New York: Oxford University Press, 1969, pp. 21-61.

Wecter, Dixon. *The Hero in America: A Chronicle of Hero Worship*. New York: Charles Scribner's Sons, 1941, pp. 415-444.

Wright, Elsie. *Boy's Book of Famous Fliers*. New York: World Publishing, 1951, pp. 64-106.

Articles and Editorials in Journals and Magazines

Adams, James T. "What Does Colonel Lindbergh Believe?" *Current History and Forum* 52 (September 1940):17-18.

Allen, Carl B. "The Facts About Lindbergh." *Saturday Evening Post* 213 (28 December 1940):12-13 and 50-53.

_____. "Lindbergh: Ambassador of Flight." *Aerospace International* 3 (May/June 1967):10-11.

Allen, Richard S. "The Lockheed Sirius." *American Aviation Historical Society Journal* (Winter 1965):266-280.

"Aloof Lone Eagle: Lindy Shuns Air Show." *U.S. News* 62 (1 May 1967):24.

"American Epic." *Time* 62 (14 September 1953):116ff.

"American Viking of the Air." *Outlook* 146 (1 June 1927):139-140.

"An Attempt to Recapture the Thrill of Lindbergh's Flight to Paris." *U.S. Air Services* 37, no. 5 (May 1952):5-6.

Baker, R. "The Hick." *New York Times Magazine*, 29 September 1974, p. 6.

Bamford, MSgt. Hal. "Prologue to Fame." *Airman Magazine* 3 (January 1959):43-44.

Barnes, H. E. "Deeper Lesson of the Lindbergh Kidnapping." *Survey* 68 (1 April 1932):17-19.

Barrett, D. F. "Insurance Aspects of Lindbergh's Flight." *National Underwriter* 59 (15 December 1955):15ff.

"Behind the Empty Crib." *Christian Century* 49 (16 March 1932):343-345.

Bent, Silas. "Lindbergh and the Press." *Outlook* 160 (April 1932):212-214ff.

Berg, L. "Lone Eagle." *Commentary* 51 (February 1971):95-98. [Reply with rejoinder: I. M. Engel, *Commentary* 52 (July 1971):30.]

Bing, Richard J. "The Public Knew Lindbergh as a Pilot, but He Explored Science, Too." *Los Angeles Times*, 25 September 1974, 5:1-4.

"Biography." *Current Biography* 15 (January 1954):37-40. Also in *Current Biography Yearbook 1954*, 410-413.

"Biography." *National Cyclopedia of American Biography* 60 (1981):325-327.

Black, Lynn S. "The Lindbergh Story." *Aero Digest* 64, no. 5 (May 1952):42-56 and 62-86.

Blackinton, A. H. "Photographing Lindbergh for the Press." *American Photography* 22 (December 1928):668-680.

Bowers, Peter M. "The Many Splendid 'Spirits of St. Louis.' " *Air Progress* 20 (June 1967):15-18 and 70-72.

Bowman, Pierre. "The 'Lone Eagle's' Last Flight." *Reader's Digest* 105 (December 1974):255-258, 260.

"Boy's Leading Hero." *Literary Digest* 96 (11 February 1928):31-32.

Broun, Heywood H. "Ambassador's Pajamas." *New Republic* 100 (1 November 1939):365-366.

Brown, K. V. "Flight that Tied the World Together." *Popular Mechanics* 127 (May 1967):84-87.

Bruno, Harry A., and William S. Dutton. "Lindbergh the Famous Unknown." *Saturday Evening Post* 206 (21 October 1933):23ff.

_____. "Why Slim Flew to Paris." *Aerospace Historian* 14 (Autumn 1967):144-145.

Buckley, William F., Jr. "Old Debate." *National Review* 22 (22 September 1970):1017.

Butterfield, Roger. "Lindbergh: Stubborn Young Man of Strange Ideas Becomes a Leader of Wartime Opposition." *Life* 11 (11 August 1941):64-70.

Butz, J. S., Jr. "New York to Paris: How Lindbergh Did It." *Aerospace International* 3 (May/June 1967):20-21ff.

Carter, Dustin W. "Reflections on 'Lindy.' " *American Aviation Historical Society Journal* 22 (Spring 1977):10-11.

Chakravorty, Ranes C. "Charles A. Lindbergh: Bioengineer and Biologist." *Scalpel and Tongs* 21 (Summer 1977): pages unknown. (I saw an unpaginated photocopy of this article in the Minnesota Historical Society Collection at St. Paul, Minnesota, but have been unable to find it in any index or reference to confirm page numbers.)

Chamberlain, J. "Adventure in Honesty." *National Review* 22 (17 November 1970):1213-1214.

———. "Lindbergh Was of the Twenties." *National Review* 29 (27 May 1977): 608-610ff.

"Charles Augustus Lindbergh." *Washington Post*, 27 August 1974, A18:1-2. (Editorial at Lindbergh's death.)

Chelminski, Rudolph. "The Lindberghs Liberate Monkeys from Constraints." *Smithsonian* 7 (March 1977):59-64.

"Child Murder as Entertainment." *Catholic World* 140 (March 1935):641-644.

Clemons, W. "Head in the Clouds." *Newsweek* 91 (13 February 1978):92-93.

Collins, Frederick L. "Why Lindbergh Acted That Way." *Liberty* 18 (7 June 1941): 16-17 and 46-47; (14 June):18-19ff; (21 June):18-19ff; (28 June):34-36.

Collins, Michael. "Showing Lindbergh the Air and Space Museum." *Saturday Review* 4 (16 April 1977):30-31ff.

"Colonel Lindbergh's Homecoming." *Aero Digest* (July 1927):31-32ff.

"Commemorating the Twenty-fifth Anniversary of Lindbergh's New York-Paris Flight." *Aero Digest* 64 (May 1952):17-86. (Articles by DeWitt C. Ramsey, Lauren D. Lyman, George F. McLaughlin, and Lynn S. Black: listed individually in this checklist.)

Considine, Bob. "Aloha Lindy." *Air Line Pilot* (May 1977):32-33.

Coughlin, G. "When Lindbergh Saved the Day for Me: First Plane-to-Ground Commercial Radio Message." *Reader's Digest* 72 (February 1958):81-84.

Courtney, W. B. "Real Lindbergh: Interview with H. H. Perkins." *Collier's* 90 (16 July 1932):10-11ff.

Craig, J. B. "Wood Wizard: Tracking Down Lindbergh Kidnapper by Wood Analysis." *American Forests* 73 (October 1967):28-30ff.

Crawford, Kenneth. "Charles Augustus Lindbergh: A Life of Superlatives." *Washington Post*, 27 August 1974, C3:1-8.

Davidson, David. "The Story of the Century." *American Heritage* 27 (February 1976):23-29ff. (On the Lindbergh kidnapping.)

Davidson, Jesse. "The Plane that Flew to Paris." *Model Airplane News* 16 (June 1937):4-7ff.

Davis, Richard. "Aviation: Lindbergh Still Solos in Anonymity." *Newsweek* 34 (5 December 1949):23-25.

Delear, Frank J. "Charles Lindbergh: A Closer Look." *American Aviation Historical Society Journal* 26 (Winter 1981):304-310.

Dempewolff, R. F. "Flight to Remember." *Popular Mechanics* 147 (May 1977):81-83.

DeSeversky, Alexander P. "Why Lindbergh Is Wrong." *American Mercury* 52, no. 209 (May 1941):519-532.

DeVoto, Bernard. "Easy Chair: Ideas About Foreign Policy." *Harper's Magazine* 188 (January 1944):141-144.

———. "Image of Napoleon." *Harper's Magazine* 183 (July 1941):221-224.

Drake, F., and K. Drake. "Thrill that Swept the World." *Reader's Digest* 52 (June 1948):7-12.

Eaker, Lt. Gen. Ira C. "The Lindbergh I Knew." *Aerospace Historian* 24 (December 1977):240-242.

Edwards, A. J. "The Plane Colonel Lindbergh Used." *Slipstream* (July 1927): 13-14.

"English Garden: Lindbergh's Idyl." *Literary Digest* 123 (9 January 1937):10-12.

Erskine, John. "Flight: Some Thoughts on the Solitary Voyage of a Certain Young Aviator." *Century Magazine* 114 (September 1927):514-518.

Ervine, St. John. "Privacy and the Lindberghs." *Fortnightly Review* 145, new series 139, (February 1936):180-186.

Evans, Raymond. "Lindbergh at the Capitol." *Outlook* (22 June 1927):243-245.

"Fame and Privacy." *Nation* (20 August 1930):195-196. (Editorial on Lindbergh's relationship with the press.)

"Family Seeks Safety." *Literary Digest* 121 (4 January 1936):27-28.

"First Flight: Symposium." *Flying* 101 (September 1977):66-98ff.

Footlick, J. K., and S. Agrest. "Did Hauptmann Do It?" *Newsweek* 88 (6 December 1976):64.

"Forbidden Theme." *Christian Century* 58 (24 September 1941):1167-1169. (Concerning Lindbergh's antiwar speeches.)

Fredette, Raymond H. "Lindbergh and Munich: A Myth Revived." *The Bulletin,* Missouri Historical Society, St. Louis, Missouri (April 1977):197-202.

"From the Files: Lindbergh's Historic Story Told by NAA Records." *National Aeronautics* 15 (June 1937):7-8ff.

Gann, Ernest K. "Thirty-three Hours that Changed the World." *Saturday Review* 4 (16 April 1977):7-10.

———. "Wine of the Gods." *Saturday Review* 36 (12 September 1953):35.

Gephardt, T. "Lindbergh Stood As a Hero in an Age with Too Few Heroes." *Biography News* 1 (October 1974):1164-1165.

Giffard, K. N. "The Lone Eagle." *Navigator* 24 (Winter 1977):12-13.

Gilbert, J. "Those Early Airplanes." *Flying* 89 (December 1971):34-40ff.

Gillis, J. M. "Lowest Depths of Controversy: Reply to H. Bruno." *Catholic World* 153 (August 1941):520-522. (Concerning Lindbergh's antiwar views.)

"Going Back Time." *New York Times,* 9 April 1972, 5:1-2. (Concerning Lindbergh's interest in the Tasaday, a Stone-Age civilization in the Philippines.)

Goldwater, B. "Lone Eagle's Concern for the Bald Eagle." *Saturday Review* 53 (3 October 1970):31-32ff.

Green, Murray. "A Strange Encounter—Charles Lindbergh and Howard Hughes." *Aerospace Historian* 26 (June 1979):81-82.

Gregory, J. S. "What's Wrong with Lindbergh?" *Outlook* 156 (3 December 1930): 532-534. (Concerning Lindbergh's encounters with the press.)

Grierson, John. "Charles A. Lindbergh—A Hero Remembered." *Aerospace* 2 (October 1975):12-23. (The Lindbergh Memorial Lecture delivered on 21 May 1975 in London before the Royal Aeronautical Society—published in London.)

Hall, Donald A. "Special Facts and Figures on 'Spirit of St. Louis.' " *Slipstream* (July 1927):15.

_____. "Technical Preparation of the Airplane 'Spirit of St. Louis.' " U.S. National Advisory Committee for Aeronautics. Technical note no. 257, 1927.

Hall, George M. "When Honor Conflicts with Duty." *Air University Review* 31 (September-October 1980):45-60.

Hallion, Richard P., Jr. "Charles Augustus Lindbergh." *Astronautics and Aeronautics* (October 1974):65. (Obituary article.)

Hart, Joseph K. "O Pioneer!" *Survey* 58 (1 July 1927):384-385.

Hart, Rufus R. "A By-Product of Hazard." *USA Aviation Digest* 10 (February 1964):30-32.

"Hero and Herod: Lindbergh Flight." *Time* 27 (6 January 1936):34-36ff and (13 January 1936):27.

"High and Fast: Lindbergh's Inspection Tour." *Time* 33 (8 May 1939):15-16. (Concerning Lindbergh's inspection of U.S. airplane industry plants for General H. H. Arnold and the War Department.)

"High Cost of Fame." *New Republic* (12 June 1929):87-88. (Editorial on Lindbergh's dealings with the press.)

Hinton, Walter. "What Lindbergh Is Doing for Aviation." *Outlook* 146 (22 June 1927):246-249.

Hoar, W. P. "Two Generations of Heroism: Lindbergh." *American Opinion* 20 (May 1977):1-8ff.

Horsfall, Jessie E. "Lindbergh's Start for Paris." *Aero Digest* 10 (June 1927): 503-504ff.

Hughes, H. M. "Lindbergh Case: A Study of Human Interest and Politics." *American Journal of Sociology* 42 (July 1936):32-54.

Hyman, S. E. "Lonely Eagle." *New Republic* 103 (19 (August 1940):237-239.

Jacobs, A. M. "Gentlemen Unafraid." *St. Nicholas* 54 (October 1927):959-962.

"Joyous Game of Sending Gifts to Lindy." *Literary Digest* 101 (18 May 1929):49-58.

Kaplan, H. R. "Portrait of a Hero." *Sergeants* 20 (March 1982):20-23.

Kaufman, B. "Saving Lindbergh's First Plane." *Popular Mechanics* 153 (April 1980):106-107.

Keasler, Jack. "The Search for Leon Klink." *American Aviation Historical Society Journal* (Summer 1976):92-100. (A friend of Lindbergh's during his barnstorming period and a flight pupil when Lindbergh was in Army training at Brooks Air Force Base.)

_____. "Tracking the 'Lost' Barnstorming Pal of 'Slim' Lindbergh." *Smithsonian* 7 (May 1976):58-65.

Keller, Allan. "Baby Is Found . . . Dead! Lindbergh Case." *American History Illustrated* 10 (May 1975):10-21.

_____. "Over the Atlantic Alone: Charles Lindbergh's $25,000 Flight." *American History Illustrated* 9 (April 1974):38-45.

Ketchum, W. Q. "The Cruise of the Jelling: With Lindbergh into the North Atlantic." *Canadian Aviation* (January 1934):7-9.

Keyhoe, Donald E. "Lindbergh Four Years After." *Saturday Evening Post* 203 (30 May 1931):21ff.

_____."Lindbergh Tells Future of Aviation." *Popular Mechanics* 48 (November 1927):738-744.

_____. "Seeing America with Lindbergh." *National Geographic* 53, no. 1 (January 1928):1-46.

Knight, R. A. "Trial by Fury: the Hauptmann Affirmance." *Forum and Century* 95 (January 1936):8-10. [Further discussion in 95 (February 1936):67-68.]

Kramer, D. "Lindbergh Eyes Minnesota." *Nation* 153 (26 July 1941):72-73. (Speculating on Lindbergh's political aspiration to the Minnesota Senate.)

Kusterer, M. "Colonel Lindbergh Sells Aviation." *Outlook* 147 (7 December 1927):430-431.

"Lad from Main Street." *Independent* 118 (18 June 1927):622-623. (The *Independent* combined with *Outlook* in October 1928.)

Larson, Bruce L. "Lindbergh's Return to Minnesota in 1927." *Minnesota History* 42 (Winter 1970):141-152.

Lehman, Milton. "How Lindbergh Gave a Lift to Rocketry: Excerpts from *This High Man: A Biography of Dr. Robert H. Goddard*." *Life* 58 (4 October 1963):115-118.

Levy, N. "Justice Goes Tabloid." *American Mercury* 34 (April 1935):385-392. (On the Lindbergh kidnapping.)

"Lindbergh, Ambassador Extraordinary." *Outlook* 146 (8 June 1927):171-172.

Lindbergh, Anne M. "Flying with Lindy." *New York Times*, 27 February 1972, section 4, 13:3-4.

_____. "Immersion in Life: Journey to East Africa." *Life* 61 (21 October 1966): 88-90ff.

"Lindbergh, the Exemplar." *Literary Digest* 94 (9 July 1927):29-30.

"Lindbergh: Foreign Comments." *Living Age* 333 (1 July 1927):84-85.

"Lindbergh, in the Hearts of His Countrymen." *Review of Reviews* 76 (July 1927): 2-6.

"Lindbergh, Pilot Extraordinary and Ambassador Plenipotentiary." *St. Nicholas* 54 (July 1927):722-725.

"Lindbergh, the Symbol." *Outlook* 146 (22 June 1927): 235.

"Lindbergh: The Way of a Hero." *Time* 89 (26 May 1967):22-23.

'Lindbergh and Social Progress." *Magazine of Business* 52 (September 1927): 245-246.

"Lindbergh and the Big Lie: Recognized Technique in a Propaganda Campaign." *New Republic* 105 (13 October 1941):453-454.

"Lindbergh and the Luftwaffe." *American Mercury* 82 (April 1956):93.

"Lindbergh Anniversary Number." *Trade Winds* 3 (May 1937):3-8ff.

"Lindbergh as a Columbus." *Literary Digest* 93 (18 June 1927):20.

"Lindbergh Dies of Cancer in Hawaii at the Age of 72." *New York Times*, 27 August 1974, 1:1-2.

"Lindbergh Ends Latin-American Tour." *Aero Digest* (March 1928):340-341ff.

"Lindbergh Inaugurates New Pan American Route." *Southern Aviation* (December 1931):19.

"Lindbergh Leaves." *Christian Century* 53 (8 January 1936):38-40.

"Lindbergh Names Two Key SST Defects: Warns of Sonic Boom and Upper Air Pollution." *New York Times*, 23 March 1971, 13:1.

"Lindbergh Number." *Airpost Journal* 5 (May 1934):3-32.

"Lindbergh Opposes Further SST Work." *New York Times*, 6 February 1971, 59:4.

"Lindbergh Peace." *Nation* 152 (1 February 1941):115-116.

"Lindbergh Says Goddard Held Moon Shot Possible." *New York Times*, 24 May 1969, 16:2-3.

"Lindbergh Says Technology, If Not Curbed, May Destroy Man." *New York Times*, 7 July 1970, 25:1-5.

"Lindbergh Still Pioneers." *Science News* 92 (19 August 1967):177. (On Lindbergh's medical research concerning "artificial heart" pump.)

"Lindbergh Storm." *Newsweek* 18 (22 September 1941):16-17. (On Lindbergh's antiwar speeches.)

"The Lindbergh Survey." *U.S. Air Services* (January 1934):10-13.

"Lindbergh's Central American Flight." *Aero Digest* 12 (February 1928):174 and 301.

"Lindbergh's Flight to Mexico and Central America." *Aero Digest* 12 (January 1928):14-18.

"Lindbergh's Lockheed Seaplane." *Aero Digest* 19 (July 1931):60-64.

"Lindbergh's Nazi Pattern: Anti-Semitism." *New Republic* 105 (22 September 1941):360-361.

"Lindbergh's Own Story of Epochal Flight." *New York Times*, 23 May 1927, 1:5-8; 2:1-4. (Ghostwritten account.)

"Lindbergh's Reception in Europe and the United States." *Current History* 26 (July 1927):522-538.

"Lindbergh's Survey Flight: The Equipment of the Lockheed 'Sirius.' " *Flight* (1 March 1934):187-188.

"Lindbergh's Transatlantic Flight." *Aviation Stories and Mechanics* 1, no. 1 (July 1927): pages unknown. (An unpaginated photocopy in the Minnesota Historical Society Collection, St. Paul, Minnesota.)

"Lindy: The Advance Agent of the Air Age." *Literary Digest* 96 (7 January 1928): 37-42.

" 'Lindy': America's Tailor-Made Hero." *Air Force Times* 37 (16 May 1977):48.

Lochbiler, Peter. "Famed Aviator Lindbergh Buried Near Hawaii Home." *Biography News* 1 (October 1974):1182-1183.

Loh, Jules. "Lindy, Yesterday's Famous Hero, Is Today's Quiet Pioneer." *State Journal*, Lansing, Michigan, 20 May 1962.

"The Lone Eagle's Final Flight," *Time* 104 (9 September 1974):19-20.

"Lucky Lindy." *Senior Scholastic* 109 (5 May 1977):10-11.

"Lucky Lindy's Luckiest Day." *Senior Scholastic* 90 (19 May 1967):16.

Lyman, Lauren D. "Flight That Opened an Era: A Master Stroke of Skill, Daring." *Science Digest* 81 (May 1977):32-33.

———. "How Lindbergh Wrote a Book." United Aircraft Corporation *Bee-Hive* 29 (Summer 1954):18-20.

———. "Lindbergh Family Sails for England to Seek a Safe, Secluded Residence." *New York Times*, 23 December 1935, 1:7-8; 3:2-3.

———. "The Lindbergh I Know." *Saturday Evening Post* 225 (4 April 1953):22-23ff.

———. "Lindbergh's Flight—A Takeoff for Aviation." *Aerospace* 5 (May 1967): 2-5.

———. "Operation Zero." *Aero Digest* 64, no. 5 (May 1952): 22-25. [Also published as "Lindbergh: 'Tech Rep.' " In the *National Air Review* (June 1950):5-7.]

———. "When Lindbergh Went to Paris." United Aircraft Corporation *Bee-Hive* 42 (Spring 1967):15-21.

McCauley, T. "Wings Over the Atlantic." *Fortnightly Review* 141 (February 1934):157-166.

MacDonald, Charles. "Lindbergh in Battle." *Collier's* 117 (16 February 1946): 11-12; (23 February):26ff.

McFarland, Marvin W. "The Lindbergh Dinner." *U.S. Air Services* 39 (February 1954):17-18. (Impression of Lindbergh at a dinner of the Institute of Aeronautical Sciences in New York, 25 January 1954.)

MacKaye, Milton. "The Lindberghs—First Romancers of the Air." *Vanity Fair* (October 1935): 13-15.

McLaughlin, George F. "Ryan NY-P: 'Spirit of St. Louis.' " *Aero Digest* 64, no. 5 (May 1952):26-32ff. (Analysis of engineering design and technical features of the "Spirit of St. Louis.")

McWhirter, W. "Charles A. Lindbergh: Pragmatist and Pioneer." *Time* 103 (18 February 1974):18.

"Magic of Publicity." *New Republic* 51 (15 June 1927):83-84.

Marshall, M. "Biggest Show on Earth." *Nation* 140 (23 January 1935):93-94. (On the Lindbergh kidnapping trial.)

Martin-Chauffier, L. "Inhuman America." *Living Age* 350 (June 1936):348-349. (On public's treatment of the Lindbergh family.)

Meakin, Robert. "Flying the Albatross with Lindbergh." *American Aviation Historical Society Journal* 19 (Winter 1974):242-245.

"Mechanical Heart Being Readied for Human Use." *Today's Health* 45 (September 1967):74-75. (On Lindbergh's perfusion pump.)

Meier, F. C. "Collecting Microorganisms from the Arctic Atmosphere. With Field Notes and Material by Charles A. Lindbergh." *Scientific Monthly* (January 1935):5-20.

Mitchell, Henry. "Celebrating the Lonely Drama of Lucky Lindy's Flight." *Washington Post*, 20 May 1977, B1:1-3; B2.

Mollison, James A. "My Pal Lindbergh." *Living Age* 359 (November 1940):208-211. (Sarcastic and error-ridden commentary on Lindbergh's antiwar activities.)

Montague, R. "How Not to Fly the Atlantic: an Excerpt from *Oceans, Poles, and Airmen*." *American Heritage* 22 (April 1971):42-47ff.

Mooney, Philip. "Lindbergh and the Quiet of Christmas." *Commonweal* 103 (17 December 1976):818-820.

Morgan, Len. "Lindbergh Is Gone." *Flying* 95 (November 1974):60-63.

Morrow, L. "Lindbergh: the Heroic Curiosity." *Time* 109 (23 May 1977):86-87.

Moseley, Seth H. "The Night the Lindbergh Baby Disappeared." *Yankee* 46 (March 1982):82ff.

Mott, T. Bentley. "Herrick and Lindbergh." *World's Work* 59 (January 1930): 66-72.

Muhlfeld, E. D. "Lindy's Legacy: Charles A. Lindbergh Memorial Fund." *Flying* 99 (December 1976):6.

Nance, John. "Lindbergh Helps Philippines in Saving Monkey Eagle, Largest, Fiercest Species." *The Philadelphia Inquirer*, Sunday Morning, 4 July 1971, p. unknown.

Needham, E. "Travels with Charlie." *Esquire* 75 (March 1971):90-91ff.

Newton, Wesley P. "Lindbergh Comes to Birmingham." *Alabama Review* 26

(February 1973):105-121. (On Lindbergh's visit to Birmingham during his national goodwill tour in 1927.)

———. "The Third Flight: Charles A. Lindbergh and Aviation Diplomacy in Latin America." *American Aviation Historical Society Journal* 20 (Summer 1975):94-102.

"New York Times Gets the Scoop of the Year for Kindness." *News Week* 7 (4 January 1936):30-31. (Concerning Lindbergh's departure to live in England.)

"No Honorable Alternative." *Christian Century* 58 (7 May 1941):611-612. (Regarding Lindbergh's antiwar speeches.)

Northrop, Marvin A. "Lindbergh—the Jenny Pilot." *Western Flying Magazine* 17 (May 1937):18-19.

"Notice of the Award of the Langley Medal to Charles A. Lindbergh." *Science* 66 (1 July 1927):9.

Noyce, Wilfred. "Why Men Seek Adventure." *Horizon* 1, no. 1 (September 1958):6-13. (Brief mention of Lindbergh on p. 10.)

Nute, Grace L. "The Lindbergh Colony." *Minnesota History* 20 (1939):243-258.

Oberdeck, S. K. "Lindy and the War." *Newsweek* 76 (28 September 1970):96ff. (On publication of Lindbergh's *Wartime Journals*.)

"Obituaries: Charles A. Lindbergh." *National Review* 26 (13 September 1974): 1027-1028; *New Yorker* 50 (9 September 1974):31; *Newsweek* 84 (9 September 1974):24-26; *Time* 104 (9 September 1974):19-20.

"Offer to Serve in Army Air Force." *Nation* 154 (10 January 1942):23.

Oldfield, Colonel Barney (ret.). "The Heritage of Lindbergh." *NATO's Fifteen Nations* 12 (June-July 1967):104-105ff.

Owen, Russell. "Lindbergh's 'Embassy of Good Will' to Mexico." *Literary Digest* 95 (24 December 1927):3-4.

———. "Lindbergh's Epoch-making Flight from New York to Paris." *Current History* 26 (July 1927):506-512ff.

———. "Lindbergh's Historic Central American Flight." *Current History* 28 (April 1928):89-96.

———. "What's the Matter with Lindbergh? Intimate Analysis of the Real Lindy of Today." *American Magazine* 127 (April 1939):16-17ff.

Payne, G. "Prelude to Greatness." *Coronet* 38 (September 1955):111.

Pearson, Drew, and Robert S. Allen. "Why Lindbergh Came Home." *Popular Aviation* 25 (October 1939):10-11ff.

Petrie, Valerie. "Lindbergh Transatlantic Flight: Forty-ninth Anniversary Retrospective." *Air Progress* (May 1976):72-73.

Pinchot, A. R. E., and H. Lischner. "Two Views on Lindbergh." *Catholic World* 154 (November 1941):206-210.

"Pioneer Flyer Advanced Medicine by Designing Organ Perfusion Pump." *Journal of the American Medical Association* (23 May 1977):2270-2271.

Post, A. "Columbus of the Air." *North American Review* 224 (September 1927): 353-364.

"Preliminary Plans of the New York-Paris Flight." *Slipstream* (July 1927):9-13.

"Presenting: a Guardsman! Charles A. Lindbergh." *National Guardsman* 11 (May 1957):11-13ff.

"President Coolidge Bestows Lindbergh Award." *National Geographic* (January 1928):132-140.

"President Leads the Nation in Tribute to Lindbergh." *New York Times*, 27 August 1974, 17:4-8.

"Press vs. Lindbergh." *Time* 33 (19 June 1939):20-21.

Quigley, Walter E. "Like Father, Like Son." *Saturday Evening Post* 213 (21 June 1941):27ff.

Ramsey, DeWitt C. "It Made Aviation As Well As History." *Aero Digest* 64, no. 5 (May 1952):18-21.

Rascoe, B. "Contemporary Reminiscences: the Influence of Lindbergh and Other Literary Matters." *Arts and Decoration* 27 (August 1927):58.

Rein, R. K. "Anna Hauptmann Sues a State to Absolve Her Husband of the Crime of the Century." *People Weekly* 18 (6 September 1982):34-35.

Robbins, P. "Heart of Charles Lindbergh." *American History Illustrated* 15 (6 April 1980):15.

Roberts, Chalmers. "The Spirit of Lindbergh." *Washington Post*, 29 August 1974, A30:3-5.

Rogers, SSgt Jim. "Lindbergh: An American Hero." *Soldiers* 32 (May 1977): 24-26.

Rolfe, Douglas. "From the *Spirit* to Space." Ryan Aeronautical Company *Ryan Reporter* (May-June 1967):2-7.

Ross, Nancy. "The Man Lindbergh Didn't Forget." *Washington Post*, 29 June 1973, B2:1-4. (On Lindbergh's praise of Dr. Alexis Carrel.)

Ross, Walter S. "Where Did Charles Lindbergh Go?" *Esquire* 60 (October 1963): 85-88.

Roth, Myron A. "The Week that Congress Flew." *Air Line Pilot* (May 1977):31.

"Salute to 1927 Heroes." *Aviation Week* 56 (19 May 1952):18.

Schiff, Judith A. "The Literary Lindbergh Is Celebrated at Yale." *Yale Alumni Magazine and Journal* (April 1977):14-22.

Seidman, Louis M. "The Trial and Execution of Bruno Richard Hauptmann." *Georgetown Law Journal* 66 (October 1977):1-48.

Shearer, Lloyd. "The Great and Controversial Hero." *Parade* (13 March 1977):1ff.

Shloss, L. "A Requiem for Roosevelt Field." *Pegasus* 18, no. 5 (May 1952):1-16.

"Simple Service for Lindbergh Held at Tiny Church in Hawaii." *New York Times*, 29 August 1974, 34:4-5.

Skardone, James A., and Rosanne McVay. "Flight from Fame." *Coronet* 42 (July 1957):31-43.

Skinner, Constance L. "Feet of Clay, or Eyes of Envy?" *North American Review* 228 (July 1929):41-46.

"Some Technical Notes on Lindbergh's Lockheed."*Aero Digest*(February 1934):46ff.

Sondern, Frederic, Jr. "Lindbergh Walks Alone." *Life* 6 (3 April 1939):64-75.

"Spirit Behind the Spirit." *Ryan Reporter* 18 (June 1957):15-18.

"Spirit of Lindbergh." *Newsweek* 42 (14 September 1953):110ff.

"The Spirit of St. Louis: 40th Anniversary, 1927-1967." *San Diego Union* 22 May 1967 (commemorative issue):1-32.

Strnad, Frank. "The Lindbergh Jenny Story." *American Aviation Historical Society Journal* 20 (Winter 1975):218-222.

"Supersonic Air Power vs. the Character of Man." *Flight Magazine* 41 (April 1954): 13 and 47-49.

Sutton, H. "Flight at Fifty: Symposium." *Saturday Review* 4 (16 April 1977):6-10.

Sylva, MSgt Dave. "The Lone Eagle." *Aerospace Safety*, 33 (May 1977), 2-6.

Thatcher, T. D. "Trial by Newspaper: Hauptmann Case and the Remedy." *Vital Speeches* 2 (15 September 1936):778-781.

Thomas, L., and Harry Bruno, eds. "What's the Matter with Lindbergh?" *American Magazine* 132 (August 1941):106-109.

Thompson, Craig. "Did They Really Solve the Lindbergh Case?" *Saturday Evening Post* 224 (8 March 1952):26-27ff.

Thompson, Dorothy. "What Lindbergh *Really* Wants." *Look* (18 November 1941):13-15.

Thrush, R. A. "Hero's Wife Remembers: Interview." *Good Housekeeping* 184 (June 1977):74ff.

"Toga for Lindbergh? Move Is Growing in Minnesota to Run the Flier for Senator." *Newsweek* 18 (15 September 1941):15-16.

Tozer, Elliot. "Lindbergh's Amazing Airplane." *Popular Science* 170 (May 1957): 56-59.

Train, Arthur, Jr. "More Will Live: Work of Carrel and Lindbergh." *Saturday Evening Post* 211 (23 July 1938):5-7 and 67-70.

Van Dusen, William I. "Charlie Lindbergh—Glider Pilot." *Western Flying* 7 (May 1930):50-53ff.

_____. "Exploring the Maya with Lindbergh." *Saturday Evening Post* 202 (11 January 1930):40ff.

Vecsey, George. "First Lindbergh Aeroplane Taking Shape Again on Long Island." *New York Times*,17 June 1975, 35:1.(Restoring Lindbergh's Curtiss Jenny.)

Villard, O. G. "Lindbergh and the Army and Navy." *Nation* 124 (29 June 1927): 712-713.

Wales, H. "Formidable! Lindbergh at Le Bourget." *Atlantic Monthly* 159 (June 1937):668-680.

Waller, George. "Lindbergh, the Little Plane, the Big Atlantic." *New York Times Magazine*, 22 May 1962, 42-43 and 77-82.

Ward, John W. "Lindbergh, Dos Passos and History." *Carleton Miscellany* 6, no. 3 (Summer 1965):20-41.

_____. "The Meaning of Lindbergh's Flight." *American Quarterly* 10 (Spring 1958):3-16.

Warren, Lella. "Before the Flight." *Collier's* 88 (18 July 1931):18-19ff.

Watter, Michael. "Engineering Aspects of Lindbergh's Transatlantic Flight." *Aero Digest* (October 1927):396-397ff.

Weems, P. V. H. "The Flight of the *Tingmissartoq*: The Authoritative Account of the 1933 Survey Flights of the Lindberghs." *Aviation* (February 1934):33-36, and (April 1934):102-105.

Weyer, Edward M., Jr. "Exploring Cliff Dwellings with the Lindberghs." *World's Work* 56 (December 1929):52-57.

"What Lindbergh Did for Business." *Literary Digest* 93 (25 June 1927):60-63.

Wheeler, Curtis. "Lindbergh in New York." *Outlook* (22 June 1927):245-246.

Whitman, Alden. "Daring Lindbergh Attained Unattainable with Historic Flight

Across Atlantic." *New York Times,* 27 August 1974, 18:1-6. (Written at time of Lindbergh's death.)

_____. "The Price of Fame." *New York Times Magazine,* 8 May 1977, 12-18ff.

_____. "The Return of Charles Lindbergh." *New York Times Magazine,* 23 May 1971, 28-29ff.

Whittemore, R. "Flyer and the Yahoos." *New Republic* 163 (3 October 1970):21-23.

"Who Is Behind Lindbergh?" *New Republic* 104 (5 May 1941):620-621.

"Why the World Makes Lindbergh Its Hero." *Literary Digest* 93 (25 June 1927):5-8.

Wilford, John N. "Lindbergh Memorial Fund Begun by Doolittle and Armstrong." *New York Times,* 20 October 1976, 22:2-3.

Williams, A. "I Rebuke Seversky," *Scribner's Commentator* 10 (July 1941):7-12. (Defending Lindbergh's right to dissent against the war.)

Wilson, F. J. "Undercover Man: Inside the Lindbergh Kidnapping." *Collier's* 119 (10 May 1947):18-19ff.

Witze, Claude. "Lindbergh: Did He Serve Aviation or Newspapers?" *Air Force Magazine* 60 (May 1977):40-45.

_____. "The Man at Mankind's Elbow." *Aerospace International* 3 (May-June 1967):15-16ff.

Wood, R. H. "Lindbergh News." *Aviation Week* 60 (22 February 1954):114.

Woolridge, Dorothy. "The Movies Tempt Colonel Lindbergh." *Screen Secrets* 4 (1928):26-27ff.

CREATIVE WORKS BASED ON LINDBERGH

The brief checklist that follows only begins to mirror the remarkable impact of Lindbergh's transatlantic   flight and career on the American public and the world. Together with thousands of photographs and millions of newsprint words, these were the songs, poems, films, and memorabilia that tried to capture and hold the essence of Charles A. Lindbergh—America's hero.

Musical Compositions

Besides the compositions listed below, some 120 unpublished titles appear in the U.S. Office of Copyrights. It's interesting to note that songs were written from Los Angeles to Pittsburgh and from Klamath Falls, Oregon, to Muleshoe, Texas.

Adair, Haden E. "Lindy's Flight from New York to Paris." Music by Luther Presley. New York: Frank Harding, 10 August 1927.

Ahacich, Peter. "Lindbergh Above the Clouds March." London: Stainer and Bell, 16 June 1927.

Ashburn, Mary. "Lindbergh Forever." London: Boosey and Company, 25 June 1927.

Baird, Hyde C. "The Spirit of St. Louis March." Utica, New York: The Myers Music House, 7 July 1927.

Bar, Bernard. "Lindbergh Fly On." Music by Helen K. Bar. Baltimore, 11 June 1927.

Bartlett, Carrie K. "Lindy, Our Lone Ace." Music by Robert H. Brennen. New York: Frank Harding, 20 September 1928.

Bernardi, Alfonso. "Lindbergh, a Fox-Trot." Toluca, Illinois, 28 July 1927.

Blake, William A. "Lindbergh, We Welcome You." Baltimore: Maryland Melody Mart, 24 September 1927.

Branham, Carmilla S. "Lindbergh, Ace of the Air." Music by Mary D. Switzler. San Diego: Thearle Music Company, 1 March 1928.

Brecht, Bertolt. "The Flight of the Lindberghs." Music by Kurt Weill. New York, 1959. (Libretto, originally published in German at Vienna, 8 February 1930.)

Bullard, S. Clifton. "Lindy-Hop, a Fox-Trot." Music by D. A. Cooper. New York, 18 January 1929.

Castillo, G. Y., and Roland Schofield. "Lindbergh in Havana." Music by Valero Vallve, of Cuba. Havana, 26 February 1928.

Craig, June. "The Lindy Grin." Los Angeles: Los Angeles Music Company, 2 August 1927.

Denick, Martin L. "The Lindbergh Baby." Sedan, Kansas, 13 May 1932.

Dick, Hector J. "Lindbergh, We Knew You Could Do It." New York: Frank Harding, 23 December 1927.

Dillon, Carl. "O'er the Foaming Billows." St. Paul, Minnesota, 1927.

Dring, Gertrude F. "Lindy Flew to Paris." Bellflower, California, 22 August 1927.

Eisenbourg, Adolphe. "Lindy, Lindy." Boston, 6 June 1927.

Eppins, William. "The Lindy Hop." Music by Levi Byron. Atlantic City: Christopher C. Wood, 29 July 1927.

Fauchev, Paul. "Lindbergh." Paris: Francis Salabert, 20 November 1927.

Ford, Mary. "Lindbergh." Indianapolis: Ford Music House, 7 July 1928.

Fowler, A. M. "Lindy's New York to Paree." Music by Harry Nissen. Oakland, 18 September 1931.

Fox, Catharine. "Lindbergh." London: Boosey and Company, 22 June 1927.

Frantz, Louise E. "Spirit of St. Louis." New York: Frank Harding, 28 July 1927.

Frederickson, Karen. "Lindbergh Boy." San Francisco: Gold Leaf Music, 21 July 1927.

Frey, Hugo. "Lindbergh Forever March." New York: Robbins Music Corporation, 22 March 1927.

Gaskill, Clarence. "Lindy, Anne and the Baby." Music by Irving Mills. New York: Mills Music Company, 11 July 1930.

Gilbert, L. "Lucky Lindy." New York: L. Feist, 1927.

Glazier, Florence E. "The Spirit of St. Louis." New York: Frank Harding, 1 August 1927.

Harper, R. L. "Lindbergh, Columbus of the Air." Music by Lois McDermand. Geneseo, Illinois, 16 July 1927.

Hartshorn, Gerda T. "Lindbergh's Romance." Springfield, Massachusetts, 7 September 1929.

Heller, Alma V. "Lindbergh." Music by David Reed. Hot Springs, Arkansas, 15 November 1929.

Henderson, Addie. "Lindy-Anne, A Lullaby." Houston, 10 September 1929.

Hendrickson, Mary A. "The Spirit of St. Louis." Music by Samuel H. Speck. Loup City, Nebraska, 21 October 1929.

Horvath, Paul H. "Lindbergh March." New York: Armand Wiesinger, 20 October 1927.

Ivine, Laurene. "Lindy." Music by Hattiebell Shields. Chicago: Gamble Hinged Music, 11 August 1928.

Johnson, Howard. "Lindbergh." Music by Al Sherman. New York: Shapiro, Bernstein and Company, 27 May 1927.

Jones, J. B. "Lindbergh Hop." New York: Southern Music Company, 12 June 1929.

Kerwin, Robert E. "Lindy, We're a Million Strong for You." Music by Seth P. Carpenter. Boston: Tremont Music, 2 May 1928.

Kirk, A. O. "The Spirit of St. Louis." New York: Frank Harding, 28 July 1927.

Klein, Anna R. "Lindy Flew Thru." Memphis: Clark Tate, 13 September 1927.

Klickmann, F. Henri. "The Spirit of St. Louis March." New York: Alfred and Company, 11 June 1927.

Koch, Anne. "Lindy Junior." Music by Klarence Kraemer. Chicago: Paradise Song-hit Studios, 28 March 1932.

Koplovitz, Arthur, and William J. Widenhof. "Lindbergh." Harrisburg, Pennsylvania: K & W Music, 9 June 1927.

Larrabee, Ben. "Lindy, America's Boy." St. Louis, 15 April 1928.

Leigh, Norman. "Lindy, Youth With the Heart of Gold." Music by George Cobb. Boston: Walter Jacobs, 1 July 1927.

Leon, Fausto. "Lindbergh in Mexico." Chicago: Ignacio Valle, 27 December 1927.

Long, J. Owen. "Lindy's Triumphant March." Sedalia, Missouri: A. W. Perry's Sons, 12 July 1928.

Lunau, Beulah L. "Lindbergh, America's Flyer." Music by Harry Jay. Steubenville, Ohio, 8 August 1927.

Lyons, Mena. "Lindbergh." Music by Eugene Platzman. Austin, Minnesota, 21 December 1927.

McCamly, Zurah. "The Spirit of St. Louis." New York: Frank Harding, 28 July 1927.

McCloskey, Frank. "Lindy." Philadelphia, 12 May 1928.

McCombs, Ralph V. "Lindy, Columbus of the Air." Music by Samuel H. Speck. New York: Frank Harding, 2 July 1929.

McKinney, Joseph B. "The Spirit of St. Louis." New York: Frank Harding, 14 June 1928.

McLellan, Daniel. "Lindy." Boston, 19 July 1927.

Main, Lucille G. "The Lindbergh Tragedy." Music by Jack Mahoney. New York: Frank Harding, 19 September 1932.

Mannecke, Hermann. "Lindbergh—Chamberlin March." Berlin, Germany, 14 June 1927.

Martorelli, Alfredo S. "Lindy, the Bird of the Clouds." Music by Nick Aversano. New York, 7 June 1928.

Minet, Valere L., and Frank B. Sheehan. "Lindbergh, the Great St. Louis." Music by Samuel H. Speck. New York: Frank Harding, 31 December 1929.

Mollenhauer, Crosby. "Lindy Triumphal March." In *The Brooklyn Daily Times.* Brooklyn, New York, 16 June 1927.

Nixon, Ted, and Elmer Snowden. "Lindbergh Hop, Non-Stop Stomp." New York: Bud Allen Music Company, 23 June 1927.

Olson, H. Elias. "Lindbergh's Voyage." Chicago, 1 September 1927.

_____. "Lindy the Man." Chicago, 22 June 1927.

Parkin, Charles I. "Lindy, He Knows His A, B, C's." Philadelphia: M. D. Swisher, 30 August 1930.

Poepping, Noel. "The Spirit of St. Louis March." Music by Donata G. LaBanca. Charles, Missouri, 30 June 1927.

Politi, Alfred. "Lindy, Mazurka." Steubenville, Ohio: Biagio Quattrocicache, 2 December 1930.

Roloff, Alfred. "The Spirit of St. Louis." London: Beal, Stuttard, and Company, 19 March 1928.

Ryan, Mrs. T. J. "There's Nothing Else but Lindy in the Air." St. Paul, Minnesota: Thoele Printing Company, 1927.

Sager, Mary G. "Lindy, the Knight of the Air." Music by Burrell Van Buren. Petersburg, Virginia, 26 February 1929.

Sandburg, J. G. "Lindbergh's Victory Song." Chicago: National Music Company, 5 June 1928.

Santarello, John, and Madeline Santarello. "Lindy: Homage to Lindy's Great Flight." Music by S. Baglione. San Jose, California, 2 January 1931.

Schuler, John G. "Lindy's March." Buffalo, New York: H. C. Weasner, 10 December 1928.

Simons, Moises. "Lindbergh March." Havana, Cuba, 8 February 1928.

Story, Oliver E. "Lindy, Lindy, How I'd Like to Be You." Boston: Crescent Music, 30 August 1928.

Svendsgaard, Zora. "Lindbergh, the Spirit of America." Berkeley, California, 18 August 1927.

Tobias, Charles, and Al Leurs. "We Know You'll Take Good Care of Lindy." Music by Al Sherman. New York: Shapiro, Bernstein and Company, 1929. (Cover portraits of Charles and Anne Lindbergh.)

Turner, L. M., and H. A. Hummel. "Spirit of St. Louis March." Cleveland, Ohio, 18 June 1927.

West, Charles F. "Lindy-Anne." Music by William Hoffman. Los Angeles: West Publishing Company, 13 April 1929.

Williams, J. D., and W. N. Moore. "Lindy's Lost Baby." Abilene, Texas, 18 April 1932.

Willis, John G. "The Spirit of St. Louis March." Ogden, Utah, 18 June 1927.

Wisterman, Fannie. "Lindy's In the Air." Bowling Green, Ohio, 16 June 1928.

Woods, Ralph H. "The Spirit of St. Louis March." New York: Carl Fischer, 11 June 1927.

Poetry and Drama

Blair, F. G. "Lindbergh." *National Education Association Journal* 17 (May 1928): 163.

Cox, George G. *Lindbergh: An American Epic.* Francestown, N.H.: The Golden Quill Press, 1975.

Crane, N. "Wings of Lead: Excerpt." *Literary Digest* 95 (12 November 1927):34.

Davis, B. "Signature." *Literary Digest* 93 (18 June 1927):34.

Elliston, G. "Lindbergh." *Literary Digest* 93 (18 June 1927):34.

Geldert, G. D. B. "Conquerors: Cortez—1520; Lindbergh—1927." *Literary Digest* 96 (11 February 1928):33.

Gillies, D. "Lindbergh." *Literary Digest* 94 (2 July 1927):32. [Also published with the title, "The Song," in *American Mercury* 104 (October 1927):16.]

Gray, A. K. "Slim." *Literary Digest* 97 (5 May 1928):38.

Herford, O. "Our Boy." *Literary Digest* 94 (2 July 1927):32.

Hooley, Arthur, ed. *The Spirit of St. Louis: One Hundred Poems*. New York: George H. Doran Company, 1927.

Hull, J. "Lament to Lindbergh." *Air Line Pilot* 22 (August 1953):13-14.

Jenkins, Keith E. *The Lone Eagle—Charles Lindbergh*. Washington, D.C.: Library of Congress, 1979. (Adaptation and dramatization of books by Lindbergh and others.)

Kanouse, William R. *The Lindbergh Bridge: A New One Act Play*. Washington, D.C.: Library of Congress, 1979.

Kenny, N. "Roar of the Crowd." *Literary Digest* 94 (2 July 1927):32.

Kobrin, S. "Who Ride?" *Literary Digest* 94 (2 July 1927):32.

Longstreth, T. M. "Flight 1927." *Christian Science Monitor Weekly Magazine* 19 (May 1937):8.

Michaelis, A. "Lindbergh." *Literary Digest* 94 (2 July 1927):32.

Monroe, Harriet. "To Lindbergh Flying." *Poetry* 31 (March 1928):300-301.

Naylor, J. B. "Pioneer of the Air." *Literary Digest* 94 (2 July 1927):32.

Neihardt, J. G. "Lyric Deed." *Literary Digest* 94 (9 July 1927):32.

Nelson, A. "Lindbergh, Charles." *Libraries* 34 (November 1929):439.

Norton, E. "To Captain Lindbergh." *Literary Digest* 94 (30 July 1927):32.

Penhale, David. *New York to Paris*. Toronto: Wild Press, 1975.

Phillips, H. I. "Flying Fool." *Literary Digest* 93 (11 June 1927):35.

_____. "Hero's Reward." *Literary Digest* 94 (9 July 1927):32.

Rebolledo, E. "Ave Lindbergh!" *Living Age* 334 (15 January 1928):109.

Rostand, M. "A Lindbergh." *Literary Digest* 93 (11 June 1927):35. [Translated by F. Snow in *Current History* 26 (July 1927):505-506.]

"Skoal! Charles Lindbergh, Skoal!" *Nation* 124 (1 June 1927):600.

Stafford, W. P. "Lindbergh." *Literary Digest* 96 (10 March 1928):38.

Turbyfill, M. "Our American Mercury." *Poetry* 32 (May 1928):65-66.

Turner, N. B. "Ballad of Lucky Lindbergh." *Literary Digest* 94 (13 August 1927):33.

"White Bird." *Literary Digest* 93 (11 June 1927):35.

Motion Pictures, Film Strips, and Recordings

American and Foreign Wars. Sandy Hook, Connecticut: Radio Yesteryear, 1965. 7½ ips tape. Six speeches by Charles Lindbergh: 15 September and 12 October 1939; 4 August 1940; 23 May, 17 September, and 3 October 1941. In Library of Congress: RSS, Reel 5.

Charles Lindbergh. Wolper Productions. Released by Official Films, 1962. 27 minutes, black and white, sound, 16 mm. (Motion picture biography of main events in Lindbergh's life.)

Come, Josephine, In My Flying Machine: Inventions and Topics in Popular Song, 1910-1929. New World Records, 1977. Sound disc, monophonic, 33⅓ rpm, plus program notes; includes "Lindbergh: the Eagle of the U.S.A."

"Epic Film of a Famous Flight." *Life* 42 (4 March 1957):104-106. (On the film version of *The Spirit of St. Louis*.)

General Charles Lindbergh: the Wisdom of Wilderness. Guidance Associates of

Pleasantville, New York, 1969. Filmstrip, 108 frames, 35 mm and phonodisc, 13 minutes, 33⅓ rpm.

Henson, Robert. "Lindbergh—or Dillinger." *Western Humanities Review* (Summer 1979):207-232. (Concerning the portrayal of Lindbergh in *The Lindbergh Kidnapping Case*, a 1976 film listed below.)

Kitty Hawk to Paris: The Heroic Years. New York: Learning Corporation of America, no date, 30 minutes, black and white, sound, 16 mm. (Account of famous early fliers, including Lindbergh.)

Lindbergh, by Leonard Mosley. Los Angeles: Books on Tape, 1978. (Eleven sound cassettes.)

The Lindbergh Kidnapping Case. Directed and produced by Buzz Kulik. Released by David Gerber Productions and Columbia Pictures Television, 1976. 148 minutes, color, sound, 16 mm.

Lindbergh versus the Atlantic. Wolper Productions, 1964. Released by Public Media, Inc. 25 minutes, black and white, sound, 16 mm. (Compilation of authentic films to present the story of Lindbergh and his solo transatlantic flight.)

Lindbergh's Transatlantic Flight. Released by Thorne Films, 1971. 3-minute loop film, black and white, silent, super 8 mm.

The Lone Eagle. Hollywood, California: Universal, 1927. Black and white, silent, 35 mm.

The Lone Eagle: Flight of Lindbergh. New York: Screen News Films, no date, 25 minutes, black and white, sound, 16 mm.

Lucky Lindy. Released by NET Film Service, 1956. 29 minutes, black and white, sound, 16 mm.

Movietone News: The Lindbergh Epic. Hollywood, California: Fox Studios, 1927. Various footages, black and white, voice-over sound, 35 mm. (Actual footage of Lindbergh's departure from Roosevelt Field and arrival at Le Bourget, plus coverage of tickertape parades and welcomes in the United States.)

The Spirit of St. Louis. Leland Hayward and Billy Wilder Productions, with Warner Brothers Pictures, 1957. 135 minutes, color, sound, 35 mm. Cinema Scope. (Based on Lindbergh's autobiography, with James Stewart in the title role.)

Stewart, Jimmy. "Lucky to Be Lindy." *Collier's*, 137 (30 March 1956), 30-31. (Comments on his leading role in *The Spirit of St. Louis*.)

Memorabilia

In addition to the items listed below, literally thousands of photographs, prints, portraits, and etchings of Lindbergh exist in various locations and publications. Publications carrying his portrait range from *Time* and *Newsweek* to *Popular Mechanics*, *Scientific American*, and the *Ladies Home Journal*. He was, undoubtedly, the most photographed personality of his generation.

Barker, Edna K. *Aviation: A New Game of Cards for Young and Old*. Berkeley, California, 1928. (Notes and highlights on pioneer American flying.)

Beauregard, Maria A., comp. *Illustrations of Colonel Lindbergh's Decorations and Some of His Trophies, Received within the Year Following His Transatlantic Flight of May 20-21, 1927*. St. Louis: Missouri Historical Society, 1928.

Charles A. Lindbergh and the Spirit of St. Louis. Washington: National Air and Space Museum, 1977. (Three-view drawings of the *Spirit of St. Louis*, deposited after its last flight from St. Louis to Washington, D.C. on 30 April 1928.)

Clark, N. M. "Two Lads Run the Lindbergh Beacon." *American Magazine* 111 (April 1931):76-77. (The Chicago beacon, dedicated to Lindbergh.)

Fidelma, Sister Mary, and Walter Curley, comps. *Catalog of the Charles A. Lindbergh Collection.* Weston, Massachusetts: Cardinal Spellman Philatelic Museum, 1970.

"Honoring Lindy with a Man-Made Star: Chicago Beacon." *Literary Digest* 106 (20 September 1930):37-38.

"Lindbergh Anniversary Marked in Library of Congress Exhibits." In Library of Congress *Information Bulletin* 36 (1 April 1977):214-215. (Notes a special exhibit from the Manuscript Division and the Geography and Map Division collections.)

"Lindbergh Materials." U.S. Air Force Academy, Special Collections Branch, Colorado Springs, Colorado. (Includes letters, notes, medals, songs, and other memorabilia—as well as Lindbergh's comments as a member of the Site Selection Committee for the Air Force Academy.)

"Lindbergh Ship Given Museum at Wright-Patterson." *Air Force Times* 16 (27 August 1955):13.

Lindenbusch, John H. *The Lindbergh Collection of the Missouri Historical Society.* St. Louis: Missouri Historical Society, 1977. [Also in the Missouri Historical Society *Bulletin* 33, no. 3 (April 1977):128-192.]

Martens, Earl. *The Lindbergh Commemorative Map: A Presentation Booklet.* St. Paul, Minnesota: Emporium Press, 1977.

Nelson, Lori. *Lindbergh Historical Site Instructor's Guide.* St. Paul: Minnesota Historical Society, 1982. (Available at the Lindbergh Historical Site in Little Falls, Minnesota.)

Nute, Grace L. "A Bust by Paul Fjelde." *Minnesota History* 21 (September 1940): 294-295. (Describes the bust of Lindbergh, which now greets travelers at the San Diego, California, airport—Lindbergh Field.)

"Recent Acquisitions of the Manuscript Division." *The Quarterly Journal* of the Library of Congress 24 (October 1967):260-286. (Reports acquisition of the Harold M. Bixby collection, which contains letters from Lindbergh to Bixby and to Lindbergh's mother, 750 fan letters and requests for endorsements, flight charts, and other transatlantic flight memorabilia.)

"Two Dedications." *New Yorker* 57 (8 June 1981):35-38. (Dedication of outdoor sculpture by B. E. Evensen at Roosevelt Field, Long Island, commemorating Lindbergh's flight to Paris in 1927.)

West, Levon. *A Catalogue of the Etchings of Levon West.* Compiled by Otto Torrington. New York: W. E. Rudge, 1930. (Col. Charles A. Lindbergh, no. 71.)

6

CHRONOLOGY

1902

Born on February 4, the only son of C. A. Lindbergh and Evangeline Lodge Land, at the Land home in Detroit, Michigan. His father is a successful lawyer and his mother a teacher of science in Little Falls, Minnesota. Six weeks after his birth, the family returns to Lindholm, C. A.'s 100-acre estate on the west bank of the Mississippi River. Lives with two older half sisters, Lillian and Eva, who were the offspring of C. A.'s earlier marriage.

1905

After idyllic first years, witnesses a fire that levels his large home and destroys all his toys on the house's upper level. The fire forces his family to move into a rented apartment in Minneapolis for the winter. Contracts measles, perhaps the only reason he was to see a doctor until he was seventy.

1906

His family moves back to a hotel in Little Falls for the summer while a new house is being built at Lindholm. For his large room overlooking the river in the old house, Charles trades a smaller one and a sleeping porch. Later, he was to sleep on that porch every night, even in winter. His father, C. A., becomes a congressman for the Sixth Congressional District.

1907

Because of C. A.'s election, Charles and his mother begin to spend winters in Washington, D.C. Early pictures show him at his father's side in the House of Representatives. This is the last year in which the Lindberghs live together as a family. The girls go away to school, and his parents become estranged, though not formally separated.

1908

Receives his first rifle, a single-shot Stevens .22 caliber, from Grandfather Land. Begins carrying it on hunting trips with his father. In each succeeding year, C. A. gives him responsibility for more powerful firearms. Visits and goes on rounds with Granduncle Edwin Lodge, a Detroit physician. Hears of science and views laboratory experiments and inventions at his grandfather's house.

1910

Learns to swim, characteristically, by saving himself from a deep hole in the river near his home. His father makes no effort to save him, because he believes Charles must learn to rely upon himself and discover his capabilities on his own.

1911–1912

Travels with his mother, lives in Little Falls, becomes more interested in mechanical devices. At age of ten, builds a pulley system to move blocks of ice from the river to a storage area and then to the kitchen.

1913

Learns to drive the family car—a Ford—on the Lindbergh land, even though he has to stand up to reach the pedals. Continues to travel with his mother and is therefore an itinerant student.

1914

Goes on a two-week camping trip with his father. They float down the Mississippi from its headwaters to the family farm, killing and cooking their own food and sleeping outdoors on the way. Charles learns of his father's antiwar sentiments and championing of labor against the "money trust." Of his performance C. A. said, "I found the man in him. He has good stuff, and will stick."

1916

At fourteen, drives mother and Uncle Charles from Little Falls to California. Takes six weeks because of mechanical failures and muddy roads, but he meets every challenge. Temporarily enrolls in school in California.

1918

Leaves high school to work the farm full-time, as part of a credit program in support of the war effort. Obtains high school diploma by examination and becomes the proprietor of Lindholm. Is nearly killed while plowing, when a plowshare releases from the gangplow and whizzes by just six inches from his head. Realizes there are risks in everything worthwhile, that he "could be killed as quickly on a farm as in an airplane."

1919

Takes on a dealership in milking machines and farm engines. On one winter trip he nearly freezes to death when a blizzard catches him on the way home. But he manages to get himself and his horse back to the barn. With some hired help, he does all the carpentry, veterinary work, and other chores necessary to running a large farm.

1920

Finds farming enjoyable, but not entirely satisfactory. Wants to go to Alaska and become a flier. In younger days, he had been enthralled with the barnstormer who came through Little Falls and with an air show he had seen in Fort Myer, Virginia. Now, flying seems to combine all his interests in things mechanical, in physical risk, and in personal freedom. Parents believe he should have a college education, however, so he goes to University of Wisconsin to study mechanical engineering.

1920–1922

Matriculates, fitfully, at University of Wisconsin in Madison. Spends most of his time riding and tinkering with his Excelsior motorcycle. Begins testing the motorcycle and his own body in several schemes to speed around corners or to jump the machine onto a nearby lake. Designs and builds a motor-driven iceboat. Joins R.O.T.C. and the rifle and pistol teams. Spends summer of his freshman year attending R.O.T.C. artillery school at Camp Knox, Kentucky, and touring Florida on his motorcycle. Eventually, recognizes his future at Wisconsin is dim; failing marks and lack of interest spiral as he hangs on. With the help of a school friend, Delos Dudley, obtains information on flying training from the Nebraska Aircraft Corporation. Tells his parents he wants to quit school and learn to fly. After initial objections, C. A. and Evangeline encourage him to try. At the end of March 1922, leaves University of Wisconsin on his way to Lincoln, Nebraska. His mother moves back to Detroit, to teach science at Cass Technical High School.

1922

April—Enrolls in flying training school at Lincoln, Nebraska, paying special attention to construction and maintenance of the plane.

April 9—First flight in an airplane cockpit. Because of his instructor's reluctance to fly, receives only eight hours of instruction in next six weeks.

May—Without soloing, leaves on barnstorming tour with Erold Bahl.

June—Back at Lincoln to work in factory, decides to take first parachute jump, which cures him of a childhood fear of falling. Learns more flying from H. J. ("Shorty") Lynch.

July through October—Joins Lynch on barnstorming swing through four western states. Becomes a wingwalker and parachutist, billed as "Daredevil Lindbergh."

Winter—Stays with his father at Little Falls and Minneapolis.

1923

April—Goes to Souther Field, Georgia, to buy his first plane, a Curtiss JN-4D "Jenny." After many practice runs, he finally soloes and lands.

May—Takes off for Alabama and Mississippi. Ruins a propeller in landing into a hidden ditch near Meridian. Makes $250 in first try at carrying passengers.

June—Takes his father on a campaign tour of Minnesota. Cracks up plane at Glencoe.

July—Gives mother her first flight. She joins him on a ten-day barnstorming tour.

Summer—Seeing a declining barnstorming market and his need for more training, decides to join the Army Air Corps.

Fall—While waiting for news about the Air Corps, attends air races at Lambert Field in St. Louis, Missouri. After instructing two students and learning even more flying, he sells the Jenny.

1924

January—Takes Army entrance exams at Chanute Field, Illinois. Meets Leon Klink and agrees to teach him to fly. Takes him on barnstorming tour across several southern states. Earns little money.

February—In Pensacola, Florida, receives acceptance to Army flight school. Cracks up Klink's "Canuck" airplane and delays several days while waiting for parts.

February 20—Drops down into town square at Camp Wood, Texas. Takes off down street with one-foot clearance at wingtips. Smashes into hardware store window. Once the plane is repaired, takes off again for Brooks Field in San Antonio, Texas.

March 19—Arrives at Brooks Field and enlists in the Army at age twenty-two, one of 104 beginning aviation cadets.

April—Begins flight training in mornings, ground school in afternoons, and studying at night.

June—Raises class standing to second among sixty remaining cadets, with an average of 90 percent or higher. Acquires a reputation for practical jokes, which was to stay with him throughout his life.

September—With just thirty-two others, goes to Kelly Field for the second six months of training: rigid procedures in formation flying, bombing, strafing, gunnery, and photography.

1925

March—Crashes into Lt. McAllister on training flight. Becomes member number twelve of the Caterpillar Club—men who have to parachute from planes to save their lives. Lindbergh's class was the first to be issued parachutes.

March—Commissioned a Second Lieutenant in the Army Air Service Reserve. Graduates first in class; one of only eighteen remaining from original 104. Goes to St. Louis to fly airmail for Robertson Aircraft Corporation.

May—While waiting for contract and testing new planes, jumps twice from airplanes to save his life.

August—Takes job with the Mil-Hi Airways and Flying Circus at Denver, Colorado. Chance to test plane in downdrafts, air currents, and heavy turbulence while stunt flying.

Winter—As chief pilot for Robertson Aircraft Corporation lays out route for St. Louis to Chicago mail run.

1926

January—Hires Phil Love and Thomas Nelson to help with airmail. No lights on fields, people with flashlights at way stations every thirty miles, one parachute flare per plane for night landings. Also, enlists in Missouri National Guard to instruct army pilots; promoted to First Lieutenant.

April—Flies first airmail run from St. Louis to Chicago. Schedules five round trips each week, with 99 percent efficiency.

September—On way from Peoria to Chicago, first thinks about possibilities of long-distance flight, perhaps even a nonstop between New York and Paris. Begins to find backers for such a flight, including Earl Thompson, Harold Bixby, and Harry Knight—all of St. Louis. Draws up detailed plans and prospectus to obtain initial backing.

Winter—Weeks of setbacks on transatlantic flight plans. Finally, gets St. Louis group's backing to have a plane built that would accommodate a Wright Whirlwind engine.

1927

February—Wires Ryan Airlines at San Diego, California, concerning a monoplane for the New York to Paris hop. After other possibilities fall through, goes to San Diego to see if Ryan can do the job.

March—Meticulously plans for flight. Obtains Atlantic charts from navy in San Pedro. Cuts weight and increases fuel capacity of the Ryan monoplane.

May—Completes flight testing of the *Spirit of St. Louis*, which was designed and built in just two months under the direction of flight engineer Donald Hall and company president B. F. Mahoney.

May 8—Nungesser and Coli depart from Le Bourget Field in Paris for transatlantic flight, but they disappear, leaving the feat and prize still open to Lindbergh.

May 10—Lindbergh sets new flight speed record for 1600-mile flight from San Diego to St. Louis.

May 12—Arrives at Curtiss Field in New York. Combined cross-country flight times establish new world record. By now, several of his competitors have met disaster: crashes, injuries, squabbles among backers and flight crews.

May 20—After delays for weather, takes off in a drizzle from a soggy runway at Roosevelt Field. Has had almost no sleep for previous twenty-four hours.

May 21—Arrives at Le Bourget Field in Paris after thirty-three and a half hours of fighting fog, ice clouds, and an almost overwhelming need for sleep. Eats a sandwich when he reaches the coast of France—his first food in thirty-five hours. Throngs of spectators at Le Bourget nearly injure him; they damage his plane and spirit away his carefully kept log of the flight.

May/June—Goodwill trips, press appearances, state visits. Met by massive crowds in Belgium, England, and the United States. Returns to the U.S. aboard the cruiser *Memphis*. Made a colonel in the reserves. Receives more than 2 million pieces of fan mail, 5,000 poems, and medals of valor from many states and cities.

June/July—Receives $60,000 for *New York Times* articles on flight. Writes *We* at Harry Guggenheim's house in Sands Point, Long Island.

Meets many influential Republican politicians, including his future
wife's father, Dwight Morrow. Eventual royalties for *We* total
$200,000. Turns down offered films and speaking tours worth $5 million. Consigns to the Missouri Historical Society more than 15,000
presents from sixty-nine countries. Returns large sums of money to
donors, asking them to use the money for charities or to promote
aviation.

July to October—Flies tour of forty-eight states to promote commercial
aviation. Key principles: on-time arrivals, safety for crews and spectators, all flights on straight lines from point to point—carefully plotted
in advance. Gives Henry Ford his first and only airplane ride. Finishes
tour in Philadelphia after ninety-five days, eighty-two cities, and
22,350 miles of flying.

November—While discussing a United States-Mexico City flight with Ambassador Dwight Morrow, meets future wife—Anne Spencer Morrow.

December—Begins Latin American tour with flight to Mexico City,
where 150,000 people receive him. Spends Christmas with the Morrow family at the embassy.

1928

January/February—Goodwill flights to seventeen Latin American countries, ending with a fifteen and a half-hour trip from Havana, Cuba, to
St. Louis. Receives $50,000 from *New York Times* for his account of the
tour.

March 21—Receives Congressional Medal of Honor from President
Coolidge at the White House.

April 30—Dedicates *Spirit of St. Louis* to the Smithsonian Institution, where
it now hangs suspended at the National Air and Space Museum.

May—Becomes technical consultant for Transcontinental Air Transport.
Helps organize this coast-to-coast air and rail line, in cooperation with
his St. Louis partners and Clement Keys. Also signs as consultant to
Pan American Airways, working with its president, Juan Trippe, to
develop airmail service in Central and South America.

October—Visits Anne Morrow in Mexico City and Cuernavaca. They had
been seeing one another in New York City and had become engaged.

November—Conceives of using rockets and jet propulsion to improve
long-range flying. Meets Robert H. Goddard, who was to become the
father of modern rocketry.

1929

February—Engagement to Anne officially announced by Ambassador
and Mrs. Morrow.

May 27—Marries Anne at the Morrow home in Englewood, New Jersey. They leave in disguise to foil reporters gathered outside the gates.

October—Obtains new monoplane, named *Sirius*, from factory in Burbank.

1930

April—Flies *Sirius* back to New York from California. Sets new world speed record for coast-to-coast flight.

June 22—Birth of first child, Charles Augustus Lindbergh, Jr., at the Morrow home in Englewood. Rents place near Princeton and begins building a house on 400 acres of land at Hopewell, New Jersey.

Fall—Plans trip with wife over the Arctic to the Orient. Anne begins studying for third-class radio operator's license. Charles lays out route and arranges for support along the way.

November 28—Meets Dr. Alexis Carrel at the Rockefeller Institute.

1931

July 27—Begins flight with Anne north to the Orient.

August 19—Fog-bound emergency landing between Kamchatka and Japan. Damages spreader between pontoons, but without personal injuries.

September—While flying supplies to relieve starving victims of floods in China, the Lindberghs are nearly capsized. Charles scares off crowd by firing a revolver over their heads. The *Sirius* is damaged and sunk in Hankow harbor but is eventually salvaged and shipped to California for repairs.

October 5—Anne's father, Dwight Morrow, dies of a stroke at fifty-eight. Lindberghs return to Englewood to stay with Mrs. Morrow.

1932

February—The Lindberghs move into their new home near Hopewell, New Jersey, but continue to spend most weekdays at Englewood.

March 1—Charles Lindbergh, Jr., is kidnapped, sparking a series of offers to obtain the baby's release. Dr. John F. ("Jafsie") Condon apparently makes contact with kidnappers on March 9. False leads and disappointments follow.

May 12—Baby found in shallow grave about a mile from the Lindbergh home. Autopsy shows fractured skull, apparently from an accidental blow received in a fall on the night of the kidnapping. Charles identifies the baby on the following day.

June—Realizing they cannot return to Hopewell, donates the estate to a nonprofit charity for children.

August 16—Anne gives birth to Jon. Charles issues plea to press, asking them to allow his children to grow up normally and to cease publicity, but to no avail.

Fall—Begins planning a flight to survey Atlantic routes, including Greenland, the great circle, and Europe in the north, as well as the Azores, Africa, and South America in the south.

1933

Winter/Spring—Continues planning for Atlantic flights. Obtains reconditioned plane from Lockheed in California, with larger engine, better propeller, and state-of-the-art navigational equipment.

July 9—With Anne, takes off for Newfoundland and Labrador on the way to Copenhagen. Rechristens his plane *Tingmissartoq*, an Eskimo word meaning "he who flies like a big bird."

Summer/Fall—Tours European cities and heads toward West Coast of Africa.

November/December—Flies the South Atlantic between British Gambia and Natal, Brazil. Returns to United States after five-month, 29,000-mile journey. Terrain maps, weather information, and facilities inspections would become vital to Pan American's overseas routes.

1934

February—Becomes involved in a controversy over government antitrust actions against large airlines flying the airmail. President Roosevelt's postmaster general, James Farley, claims the airlines had overcharged the government $47 million, with much of the money going to "The Lindbergh Line"—Transcontinental and Western Airways (TWA). Roosevelt cancels contracts and turns over flying to the Army Air Corps.

February 12—Sends telegram to papers and Roosevelt, stressing "condemnation without just trial" and the endangerment of army pilots in asking them to do a job they weren't trained for.

March—Testifies before committee on a Senate bill designed to return air mail contracts to the airlines, after the army had experienced twelve deaths and forty-six forced landings in two months. The bill passes, resulting in a major defeat for the Roosevelt administration.

September—Bruno Richard Hauptmann is arrested for the kidnapping and murder of Charles, Jr. Months of police work trace ransom money and other clues to Hauptmann.

1935

January—Court trial of Hauptmann begins in Flemington, New Jersey. Charles is central witness on events of the kidnapping and attempts to get Charles, Jr., back. Goes to trial, disguised, every day.

February—Hauptmann is convicted and sentenced to death without mercy. Charles reviews case and decides that "there is no doubt at all that Hauptmann did the thing."

Spring—Begins work with Dr. Alexis Carrel on perfusing oxygen through organs during operations.

June—Publishes article in *Science* magazine, with Alexis Carrel, on a perfusion pump that has kept a cat's organs alive.

September—Publishes technical article on perfusion pump for *Journal of Experimental Science*.

Fall—Press continues to invade Lindbergh's privacy. Mounting attempts to get pictures of Jon threaten his safety.

December—Announces plans to move family to England, where the citizens' respect for law and order would increase the security of his family against threats and extortionists. Most editorial comment is sympathetic.

1936

January—Takes up residence at Long Barn, Sir Harold Nicolson's home in Kent.

April—Bruno Richard Hauptmann electrocuted at state prison in Trenton, New Jersey.

May/June—Visits France and its aircraft industries. Appalled at their condition, especially considering Germany's massive remilitarization.

July—Visits Germany at invitation of Major Truman Smith, the U.S. Military Attaché in Berlin, as well as German leaders Hermann Goering and Air Marshal Milch. Obtains considerable information about German aircraft development for U.S. intelligence.

September—Demonstrates perfusion pump at International Cytological Congress in Copenhagen.

Winter—Increases discussions of German air power with British leaders. Recommends high-level, night-capable bomber to Sir Thomas Inskip, British Minister of Defence.

1937

Winter/Spring—Flying tour, with Anne, to Italy, Yugoslavia, and India.

May 12—Land Morrow Lindbergh born on coronation day for King George VI. Delays announcement to British press for two weeks.

Summer—Visits Alexis Carrel at the latter's summer home on the island of Saint-Gildas.

Fall—Returns to Germany for additional surveys of German airpower. Estimates, correctly, that next German plane will be the ME-110, a two-engine fighter.

November—With Truman Smith, prepares a report, "General Estimate of Germany's Air Power" for the U.S. General Staff.

December—Returns to United States to write a book on the culture of organs and to discuss his airpower estimates with others "back home."

1938

Summer—Lindberghs move to Iliec, an island near Alexis Carrel's home, off the coast of France.

August—Airpower assessment tour to Poland, Romania, Czechoslovakia, and the Soviet Union. Sees good aircraft plants but poor rates of production and maintenance.

October—Visits Germany for third time. At a state dinner arranged by Ambassador Hugh Wilson, receives the Service Cross of the German Eagle from Hermann Goering—for the 1927 transatlantic flight and general service to aviation.

November—As anti-Semitic riots increase in Germany, criticism of Lindbergh mounts for his acceptance of the "German Eagle." Writes letters on German airpower to Joseph P. Kennedy, U.S. ambassador to England, and to General H. H. Arnold, chief of the U.S. Army Air Corps. Though Kennedy forwards these comments to the State Department, they are never passed on to the War Department or the president.

1939

April—Returns to United States, with plans to bring family back permanently. Speaks to General Arnold regarding the German Luftwaffe. Goes on extended active duty, at Arnold's request, to help accelerate and expand aircraft design and production.

May—Makes two transcontinental inspection tours for the military aviation board. After many visits to aircraft manufacturing plants, joins in recommending planes that will help win the war for the United States.

September—Makes first speech against intervention in World War II. Says we should enter war only if "absolutely essential to the future welfare of the nation."

November—Publishes "Aviation, Geography, and Race" in *Reader's Digest*. Calls for balance of power in the West, based on the English fleet, German air force, French army, and the American nation.

1940

Continues to speak out against involvement in the war, despite heavy opposition from Franklin Roosevelt and his secretary of the interior, Harold Ickes. Several of his former friends denounce him as a Nazi or a traitor. In the fall a daughter, Anne Spencer Lindbergh, is born.

1941

March—Writes "A Letter to Americans" for *Collier's*, which accuses Roosevelt of shouting for peace while he consistently directs the country toward war. Also, with Anne, convalesces from chicken pox by sailing the Florida Keys and Everglades. Reveals in his diaries his concern for nature and the continuity of life.

April—Joins the America First Committee and begins speaking on its behalf against the war. Marks the defeat of France and imminent disaster for the British. Considers British defeat a "tragedy" and says he isn't for a German victory, but feels we must stay out of a war that we are unprepared to fight. When Roosevelt calls him a Copperhead and a "sunshine patriot" at a news conference, resigns his commission as a Colonel in the U.S. Air Corps Reserve.

June—Rents house on north shore of Long Island. Old friends like Harry Guggenheim and Henry Breckenridge become estranged from him. FBI begins surveillance of his activities.

July—Harold Ickes calls him a "Knight of the German Eagle" and a friend of "a foreign government." Writes open letter to Roosevelt asking that the president set the record straight on his receiving the medal as an official representative of the U.S. government.

September—Makes infamous speech at Des Moines, naming the British, the Roosevelt administration, and the Jews as dangerous influences toward involvement in the war. Claims sympathy for Jewish persecution, but decries their influence on motion pictures, the press, radio, and government.

October—Last speech to audience of 20,000 at Madison Square Garden. Receives a fervent, six-minute ovation.

December—Japanese attack on Pearl Harbor and declaration of war cause America First Committee to disband. Issues statement on December 9 declaring full support of the war effort "regardless of our attitude in the past." Tries to get back into uniform, but is denied the opportunity by Secretary of War Stimson, unless he recants pre-war views. Decides to seek work in the civilian aviation industry.

1942–1943

After being turned down by several companies, he is invited by Henry

Ford to work on the B-24 "Liberator" bomber at Willow Run, Detroit, Michigan. Perhaps because of Ford's influence, the position is approved by the War Department. During the next eighteen months, alternates duties between aerospace medicine and B-24 design work. Conducts high-altitude experiments on himself at the Aero Medical Laboratory of the Mayo Clinic in Rochester, Minnesota. Redesigns parachute equipment and conducts tests of ignition systems in aircraft with Pratt-Whitney engines. Nearly loses his life from oxygen deprivation in one such test. Recommends key changes to the B-24, including improvements in crew armaments and redesign of the gun turrets for maximum rotation on target. Fifth child is born on August 13, 1942. Makes no public statements on political issues.

1944

April through August—Goes to South Pacific with the Navy as a Technical Representative for United Aircraft Corporation; tests F-4U "Corsair" under combat conditions at Rabaul, New Hebrides. Checks out in twin-engine P-38 fighters at New Guinea. In a borrowed plane, flies combat missions with 475th Fighter Group. Credited with one "kill" on a Sonia-type Japanese fighter in head-to-head combat. Develops special fuel-saving technique for P-38s, which increases their combat radius by 250-300 miles.

September—Demonstrates how to triple the bomb load for Corsair squadrons in Guam and Roi. Arrives back in the United States on September 16, having completed fifty combat missions and flown 178 combat hours. Continues aircraft development work through rest of the year.

1945

Spring—Asked by United Aircraft to go to Germany when the armistice is signed, in order to study German developments in aircraft and missiles. Becomes a consultant attached to the U.S. Navy Technical Mission.

May—Arrives in Paris, six days after the official German surrender. Observes bad treatment of Germans by French, Russians, and Americans. About a concentration camp near Nordhausen, observes that here "was a place where men and life and death had reached the lowest form of degradation." Becomes alarmed at Russian inroads on the German scientific community and is determined that the U.S. should overcome it. Recommends several "acquisitions" for the West, including Wernher von Braun, in his final report.

Fall—Reeve Lindbergh, his last child and second daughter, is born.

1946–1947

Devotes post-war years to development of civilian and military air-power. Acts as a civilian advisor to coordinate research on and help improve America's defenses. Establishes home on several acres of land in Darien, Connecticut, and commutes to work in New York and Washington, D.C. During time with his family, develops in his children the same freedom with responsibility that had molded his own childhood.

1948

Early—Publishes *Of Flight and Life* as reflections on the war and Western civilization. Recounts his brush with death from oxygen starvation during one high-altitude test in a P-47, which taught him "that in worshipping science man gains power, but loses the quality of life." Begins to develop his views of preserving Western culture through a balance of power, progress, and moral responsibility.

April—Reunited with Harry Guggenheim, who had continued to support the rocket and missile research of Robert Goddard, when he stands with Guggenheim at the American Museum of Natural History to honor Goddard's memory. Continues work on civilian and military aviation through the year.

1949

Early in the year, goes to Europe as an advisor to the Allied Forces on the Berlin Airlift. Takes personal interest in overcoming the Soviet blockade of Berlin: gives pep talks to crews and often rides herd on shuttle runs through the East German corridor. Upon his return to the United States, receives the Wright Brothers Memorial Trophy for "significant public service of enduring evaluation to aviation and the United States." In his acceptance speech, pleads for continual balancing of the "hothouse" achievements of science with enduring qualities of body, mind, and spirit.

1950–1952

Continues active work for aviation in support of the Korean War. Sees his early ideas about jet power become a reality in first-generation jet fighters. Supports Truman and MacArthur during the war, but votes for Adlai Stevenson (a liberal Democrat) in the presidential elections of 1952.

1952

Selected as a member of the advisory board on establishing a U.S. Air Force Academy. Expresses a number of his concerns about developing the best possible officers to command the awesome destructive forces of bombers and missiles. Believes a special cadre, developed at an academy designed for the purpose, is necessary for Strategic Air Comand crews. In 1953, publishes *The Spirit of St. Louis*, a stylistic tour-de-force recounting the transatlantic flight of 1927. Its stream-of-consciousness narrative, laced with flashbacks and philosophical reflections, establishes both his literary skill and his movement from a man of action to a man of contemplation. Wins the 1954 Pulitizer Prize for biography.

1954

April—Sworn in as a brigadier general in the U.S. Air Force Reserve, once more wearing his wings by direction of President Eisenhower. Also appointed to the Air Force Scientific Advisory Board. Increases his time at New Mexico and other missile proving grounds, as well as his association with Wernher von Braun and other ex-Nazi rocket specialists, who work to write a complete history of German rocket development. Becomes increasingly occupied with manned space flight and space medicine.

1955–1960

Anne leaves home in early 1955, soon after her mother's death, to live at a rented southern beach cottage. Feels vaguely unhappy, needing to be alone and without the demands of children. Begins a period of increasing estrangement between her and the ever-busy and well-traveled Charles. In 1957, he sees movie version of *The Spirit of St. Louis*, but refuses to promote it with personal appearances or press interviews. Continues to fly with and evaluate Strategic Air Command crews, enduring twelve-hour flights over the polar cap and even more difficult boardroom meetings.

1960–1964

Votes for Richard Nixon, but still invited to the White House by the Kennedys. Continues to work as a director of Pan American Airlines, especially advising on plans to develop a supersonic plane. Becomes more and more dissatisfied with long meetings in stuffy boardrooms and endless technical planning sessions. After one such conference in New York, he feels a sudden revulsion for the supersonic future, flies to Nairobi, and escapes into the African bush country. Writes an article for *Reader's Digest* in July 1964, in which he says "that the construction of an airplane, for example, is simple when compared with the evolutionary achievement of a bird. . . . If I had to choose, I would rather have birds than airplanes.''

1965-1970

Deepens his commitment to conservation by joining the boards of the World Wild Life Fund and the National Union for the Conservation of Nature. Takes an active role in saving the blue and hump-backed whales from slaughter off the coast of Peru. In the Christmas 1967 issue of *Life* magazine, says that if he were entering adulthood in the 1960s, he would choose a career that kept him in touch with nature more than with science, because ''an over-emphasis of science weakens character and upsets life's essential balance.'' At a Geneva meeting for the World Wild Life Fund in 1968, becomes interested in projects to save the tamarau and monkey-eating eagle of the Philippines. Travels on several difficult expeditions to the Philippines during the next two years. Balances these involvements in conservation with continuing interest in the Apollo program. Attends dinner at the White House for Apollo astronauts and sees the moon shot from Cape Kennedy. This fulfillment of Robert Goddard's dream is a great mark of contentment for him.

1970-1972

Although he remains active, these years become a time of writing and reflection on his life. In 1970, publishes his World War II diaries as *The Wartime Journals of Charles Lindbergh*, at least partly as a rejoinder to Harold Nicolson's own printed remarks about his views during the war. Begins notes for a final autobiography, which would be published posthumously as *Autobiography of Values*. During 1972, has his last great adventure on an expedition to find the primitive Tasadays, a Stone-Age tribe of Mindanao Island, in the Philippines. Fascinated by this tribe of people, who had no contact with outsiders until the late 1960s and no words in their language for war, enemy, murder, or moral badness. Obtains proclamation from President Ferdinand Marcos to protect more than 46,000 acres of Tasaday country as a reserve.

1973-1974

Spends most of 1973 reaching into the past: at dedication ceremonies for Harry Guggenheim's estate in Long Island; in more frequent and longer visits to his hideaway in Maui; writing to old friends he hasn't seen since before World War II; dedicating the Lindbergh farm at Little Falls, Minnesota, as a state park; and in many visits to see his plane and papers at the Smithsonian Institution. Comes down with a fever, rash, and loss of weight in the fall. Goes to Maui in spring of 1974 to recuperate, but spends the summer in failing health at his home in Darien, Connecticut. When he realizes the end is near, makes arrangements to be flown to Maui for burial. Dies on August 26, 1974, and is buried three hours later in the cemetery next to a little Congregational Church, overlooking the sea.

INDEX

combat, in South Pacific, 31, 137;
and commercial aviation, 15-19,
22-23, 34-35, 43-48, 88-90; death
and burial, 37, 141; education, 5-6,
127-28; family background, 1-3,
125-27 (see also Boyhood on the
Upper Mississippi); and farming, 5-6,
127; flights, 16-17, 19-20, 22, 45-46,
88-90, 131-34 (see also Transatlantic
flight); intelligence activities, 25-27,
48, 134-35; marriage, 17, 132; mechanical genius, 5, 126-27; memorabilia, 61, 123-24; and military aviation, 25-27, 31-33, 48-50, 137;
motion picture films based on,
56-59; music based on, 59-60,
118-21; obituaries of, listed, 115;
and the Philippines, 36, 85, 95, 140;
photographs of, 56, 63-64, 71, 73,
75-77; and physical courage, 2-3, 5,
6; poetry based on, 60-61, 121-22;
and the press, 54-56, 93-94; and
science, 3, 18-19, 31, 94-95, 126,
137, 138, 140. Works: 97-101; An
Autobiography of Values, 82; Boyhood
on the Upper Mississippi, 82; The
Culture of Organs, 27, 83; forewords
and prefaces, 84-85; Of Flight and
Life, 33, 81; The Spirit of St. Louis,
34, 81-82; Wartime Journals, 81; We,
15, 81, 130-31
Lindbergh, Charles Augustus, Jr.:
birth of, 18; kidnapping of, 20-22,
90-91, 132
Lindbergh: A Biography (Mosley), 86
Lindbergh Historic Site, 80-81. See
also Lindholm
Lindbergh, Jon, 22, 25, 32, 55
The Lindbergh Kidnapping Case (film),
58-59
Lindbergh State Park and Interpretive
Center. See Lindbergh Historic Site
Lindholm, as Lindbergh's boyhood
home, 3-4, 125, 127
Listen! The Wind (Lindbergh, Anne),
22
Little Falls, Minnesota, 2-4, 50-51, 80,
125-27

Love, Phil, 10-11, 129
Lyman, Lauren D., 13, 25, 55, 94
Lynch, H. J. ("Shorty"), 8, 128

Manson, Ola. See Lindbergh, August
Mechanical heart. See Perfusion
pump
Media. See Motion picture films;
Newsprint journalism
Medical research. See Carrel, Alexis;
Lindbergh, Charles Augustus, and
science; Perfusion pump; Space pro-
gram, U.S.
Memorabilia: of Lindbergh's career,
61; list of, 123-24
Mexico City, 16, 17, 89
Military aviation. See Aviation,
military
Military power. See Aviation, military;
Europe: airpower, during World
War II; Intervention, in World War
II; Missiles, and ballistic missile
defense; Strategic Air Command
(SAC)
Minnesota Historical Society, Lind-
bergh holdings, 80
Missiles, and ballistic missile defense,
33-34, 49, 139
Missouri Historical Society, Lindbergh
holdings, 80
Morrow, Anne. See Lindbergh, Anne
Morrow
Morrow, Dwight, 16, 89, 131, 132
Morrow, Elizabeth, 19
Mosley, Leonard, 16, 86
Motion picture films about Lindbergh,
56-59; listed, 122-23
Movietone News, 56-57
Music, based on Lindbergh: discus-
sion of, 59-60; list of, 118-21

NACA (National Advisory Committee
for Aeronautics). See NASA
NASA (National Aeronautics and Space
Administration), 27 (NACA), 47
Nature, Lindbergh's appreciation of,
4-5, 35-36, 50-51, 95, 140
Nazism, Lindbergh's purported asso-

About the Author

PERRY D. LUCKETT is Associate Professor of English at the United States Air Force Academy, specializing in American studies. He has published articles in the *Journal of American Culture* and the *Journal of Popular Culture*.